Cool Santa

Christmas Coloring Book

Get ready for **Master Rabbit** designed *Cool Coloring Book* series with this cute festive **Cool Santa Christmas Coloring Book**!

A great way to celebrate the holidays with your little ones is to use this big coloring book to give them first hand festive feeling. To color the imaginative Santa in this coloring book can help them to build fine-motor skills and hand-eye coordination. Spectacular designs for all different looking Santa Clause accompanied by snowmen, unicorns, Christmas trees, presents, toys, stockings, and more!

No matter you are at which level of coloring, or even for little kids, this book will give you a lot of fun. Like **Master Rabbit**'s other *Cool Coloring Book* series, each of the Santas in the design is wearing a pair of cool sunglasses.

Features:

- 25 different images with duplication of each, so you can color in different themes.
- Printed single side for no bleed through.
- Large 8.5 x 11 pages.
- Perfect Christmas coloring book for kids of all ages or even adults.
- Can be used as a Christmas gift or party favor.

Enjoy this coloring book to enlighten the kids, and expand their creativeness playing around with different color combinations. Click to buy right away!

Any question or suggestion is welcome!
Email: brothertuzi@gmail.com
Instagram: @masterabbitu

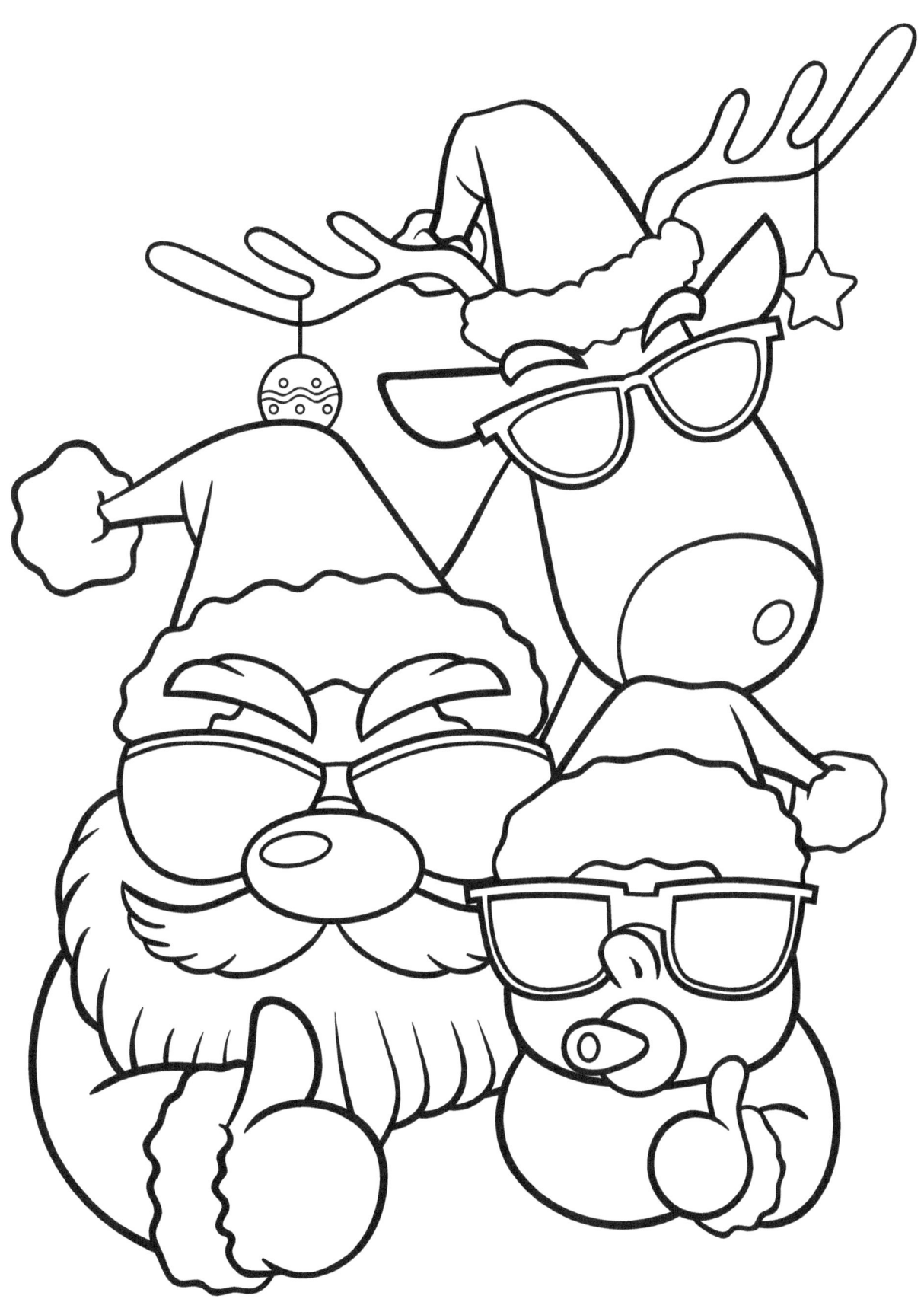

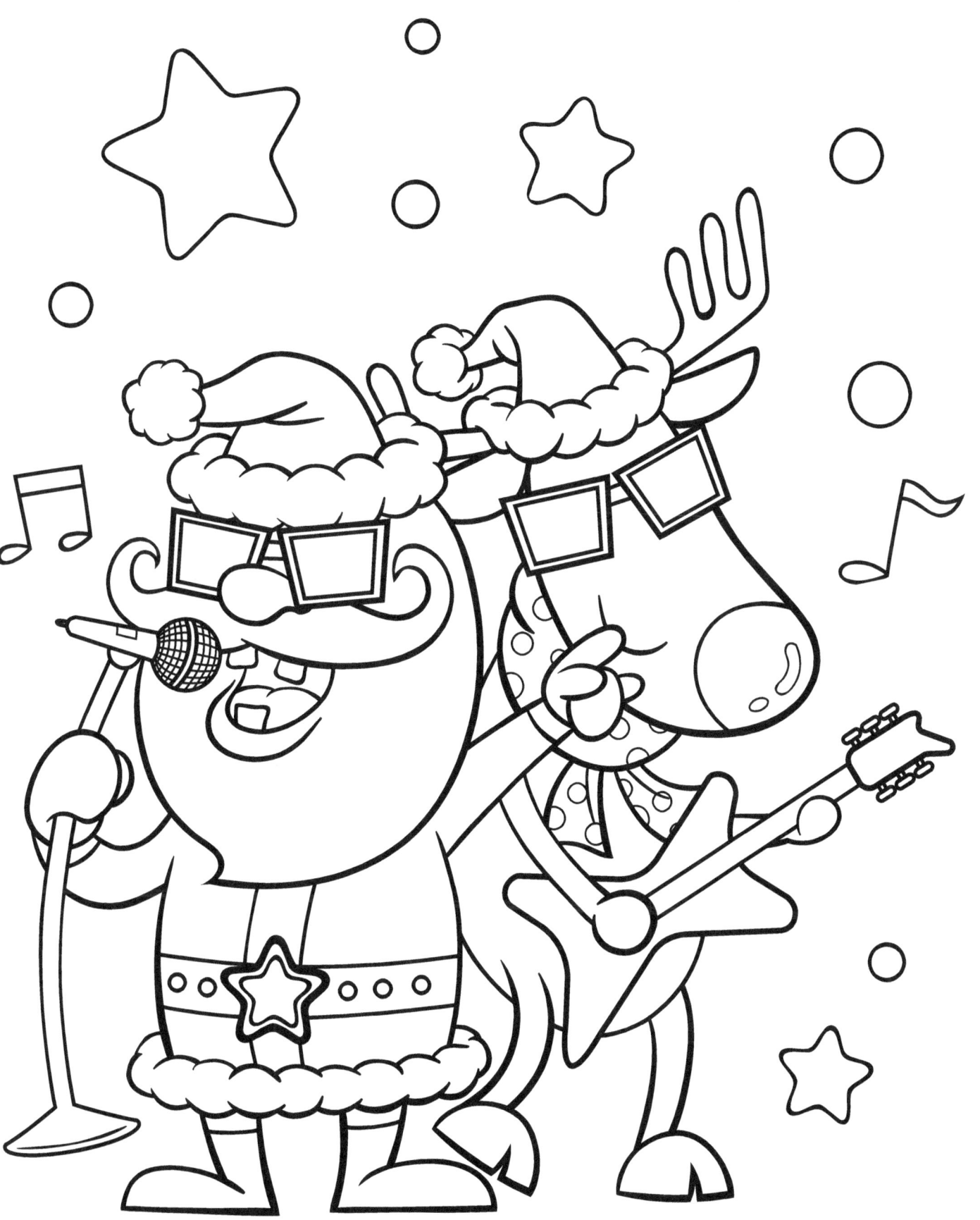

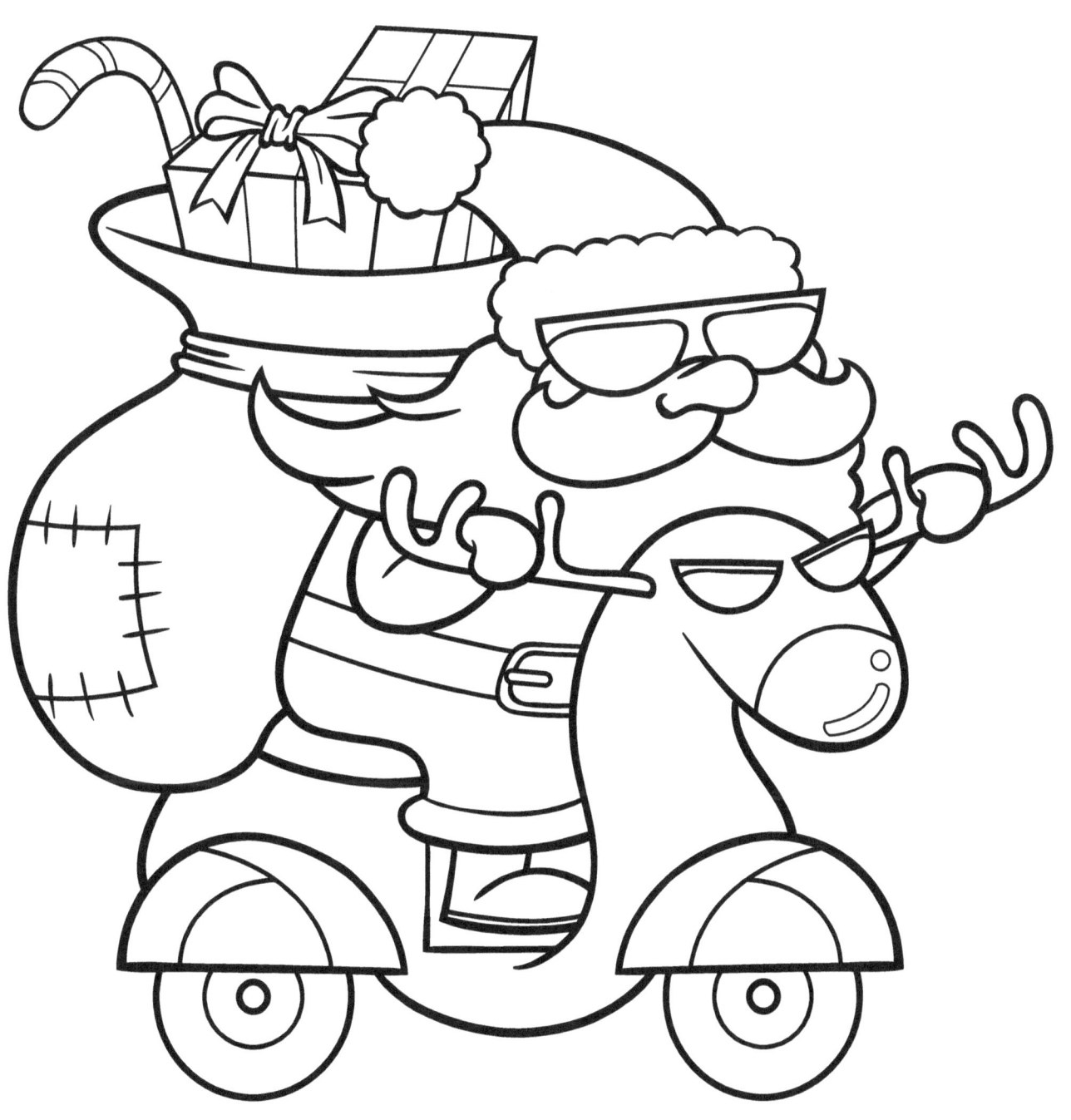

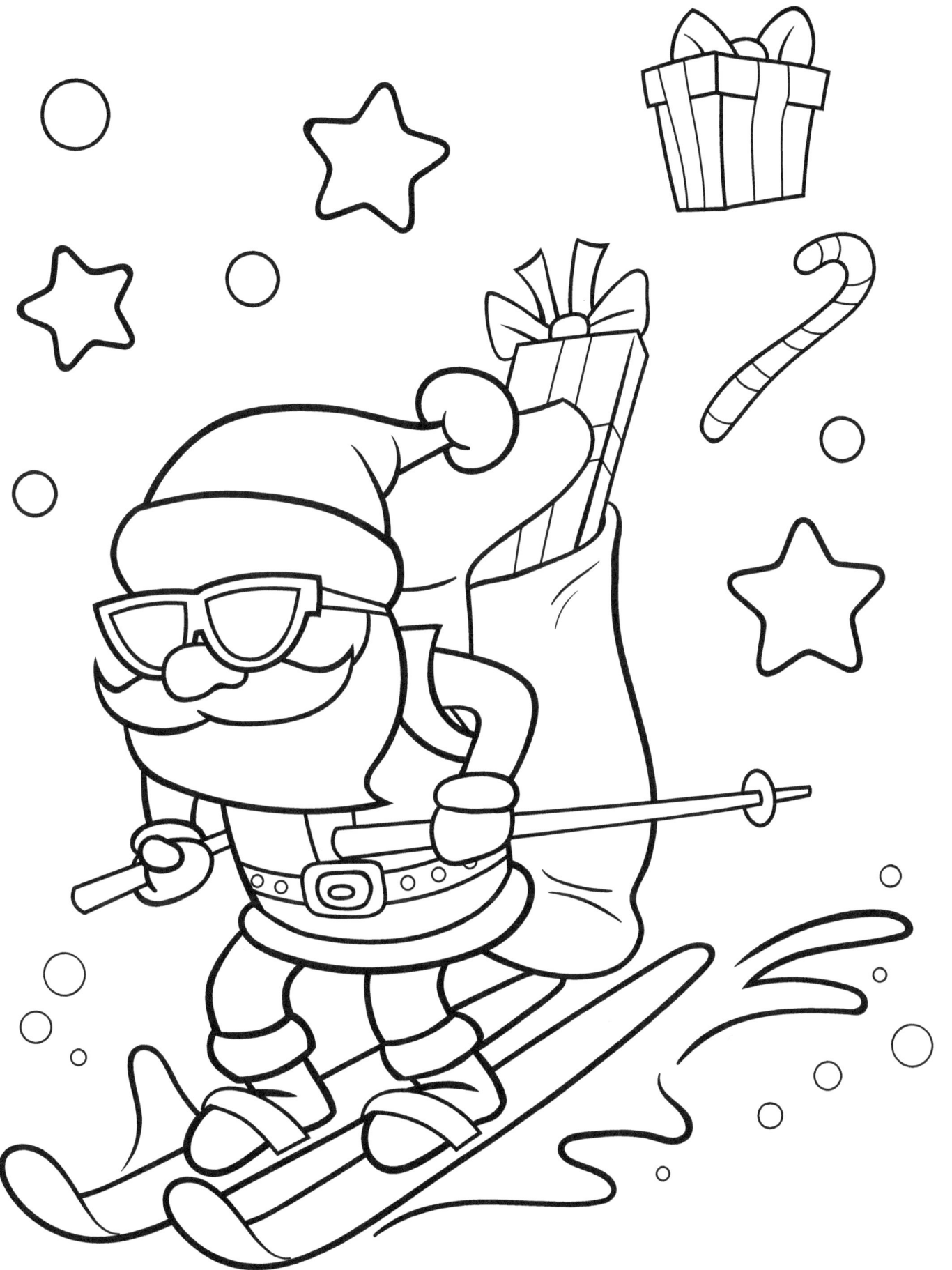

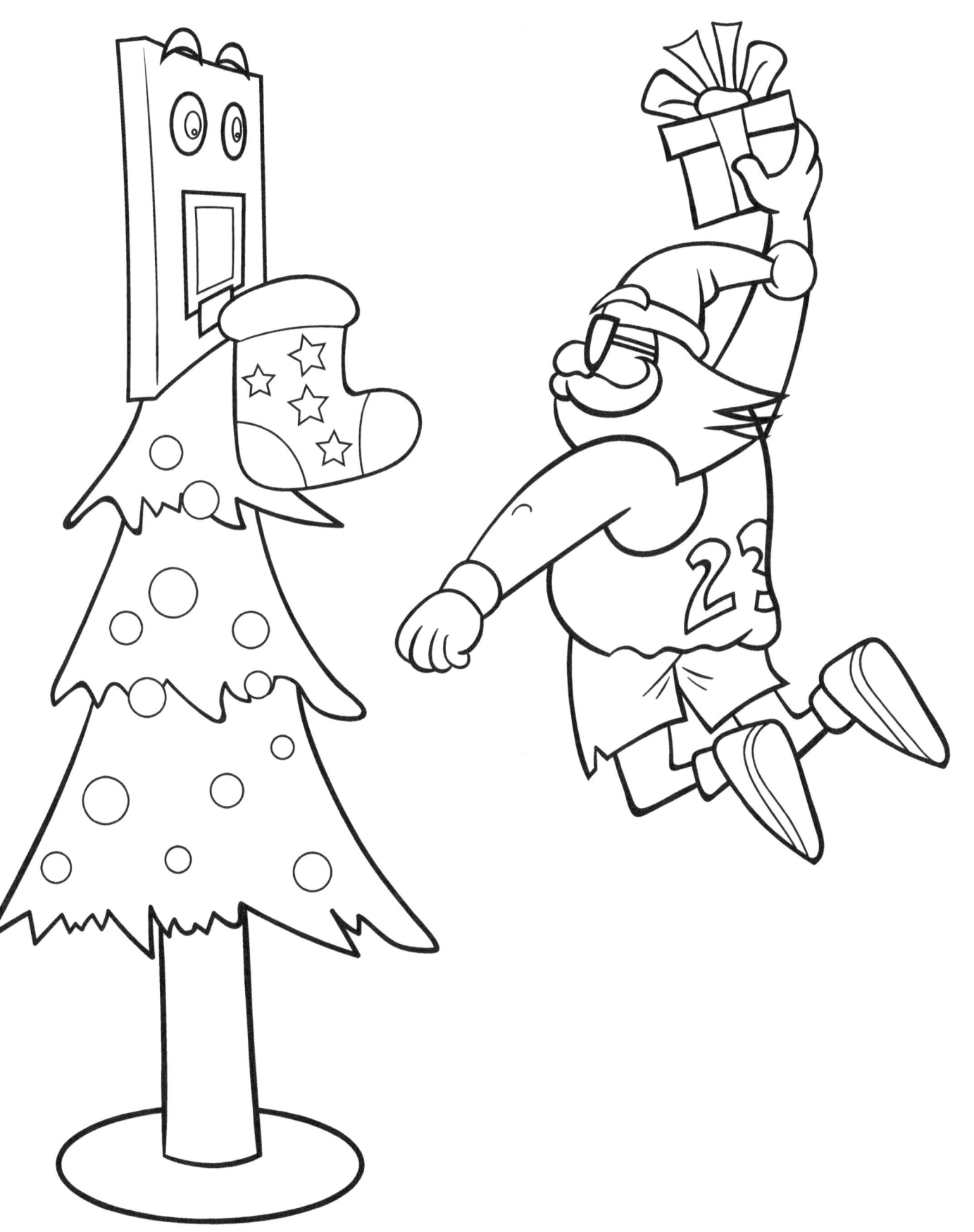

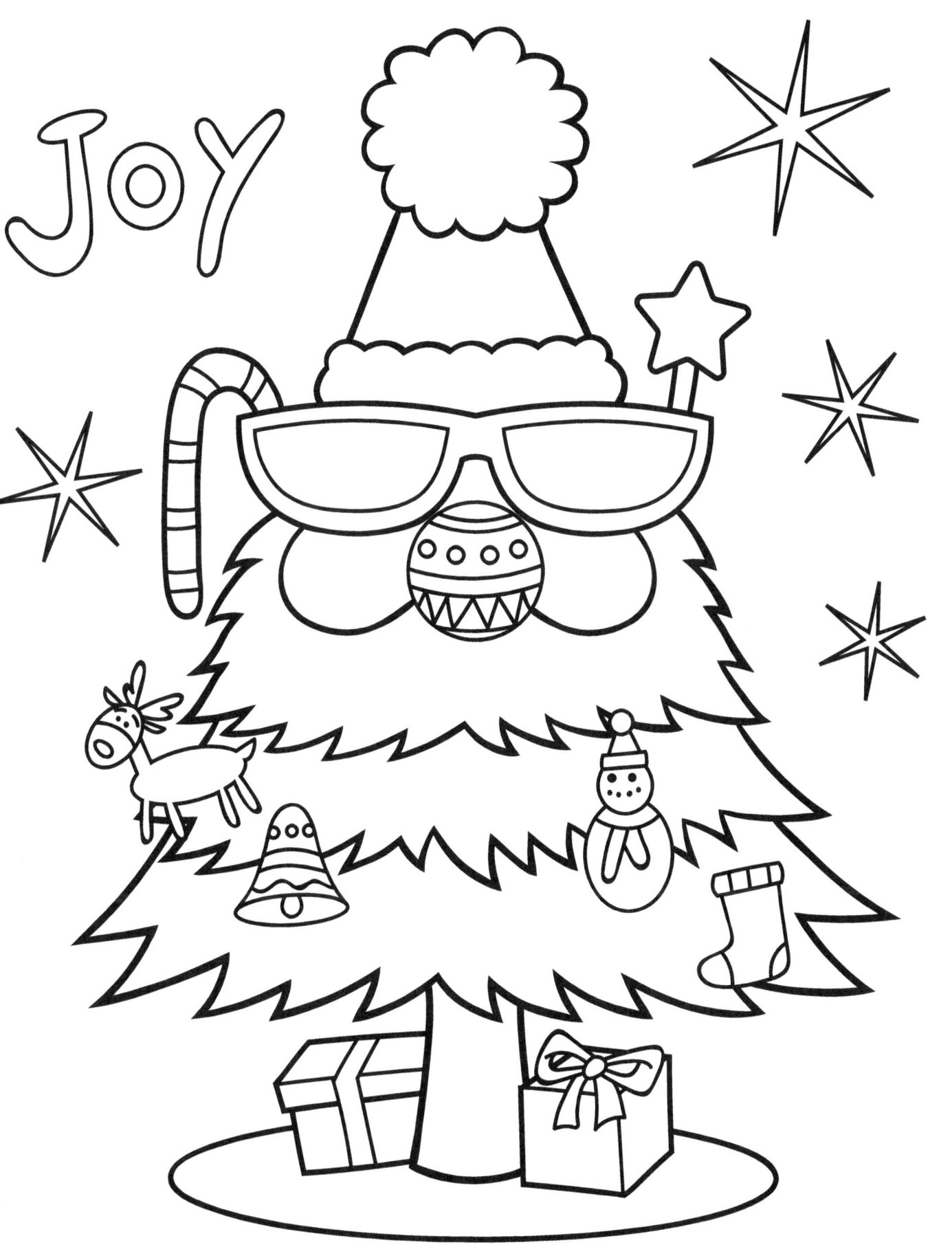

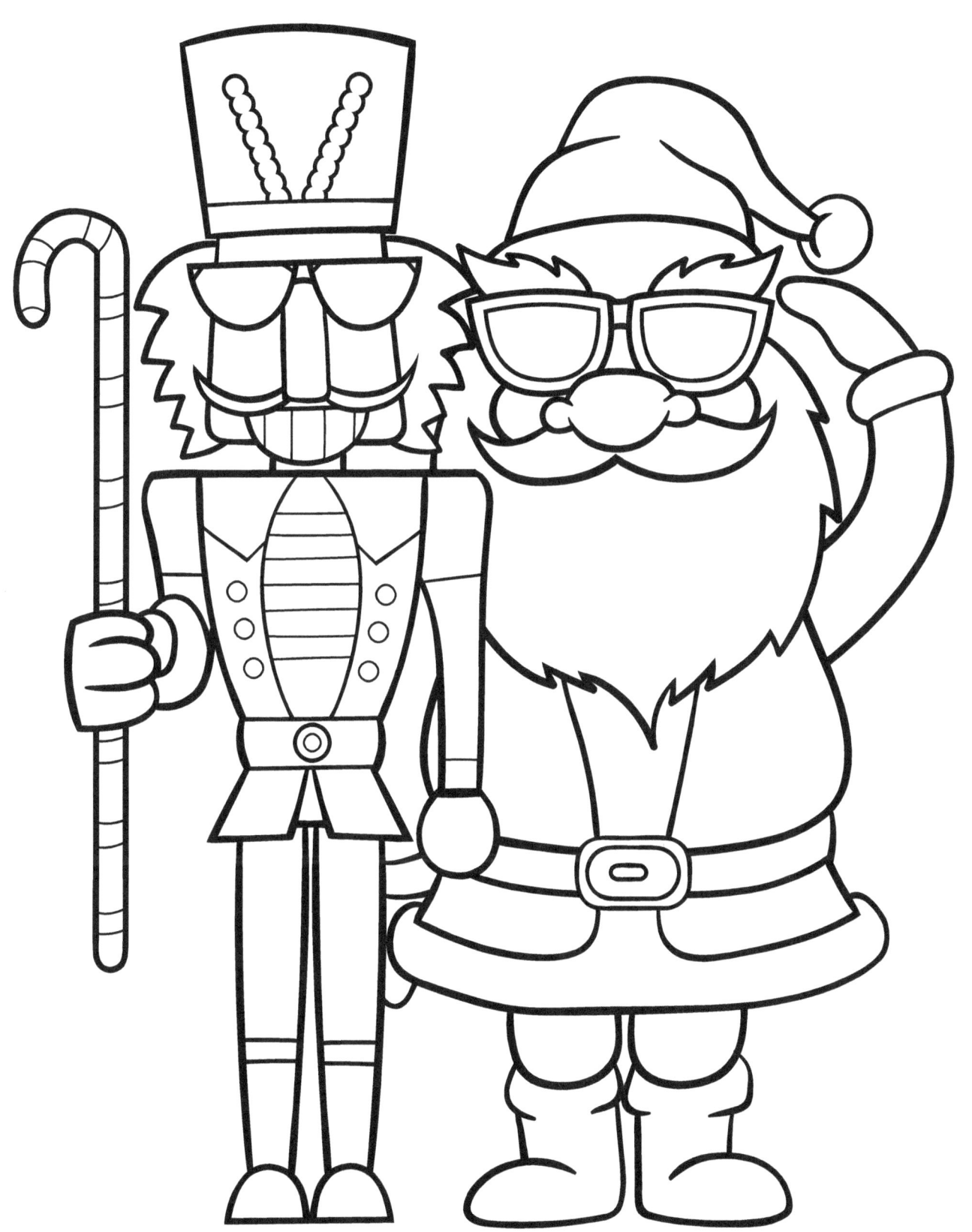

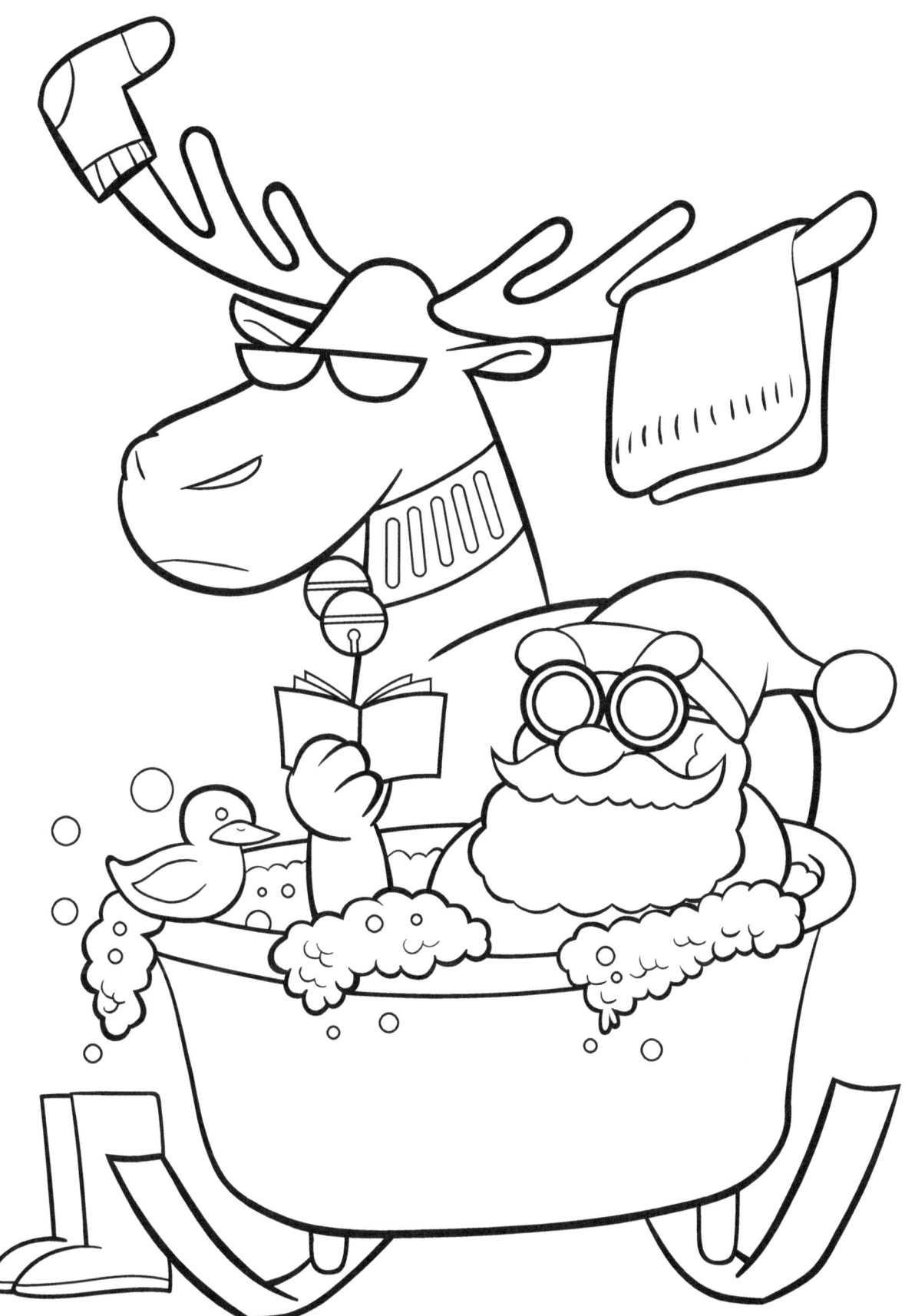

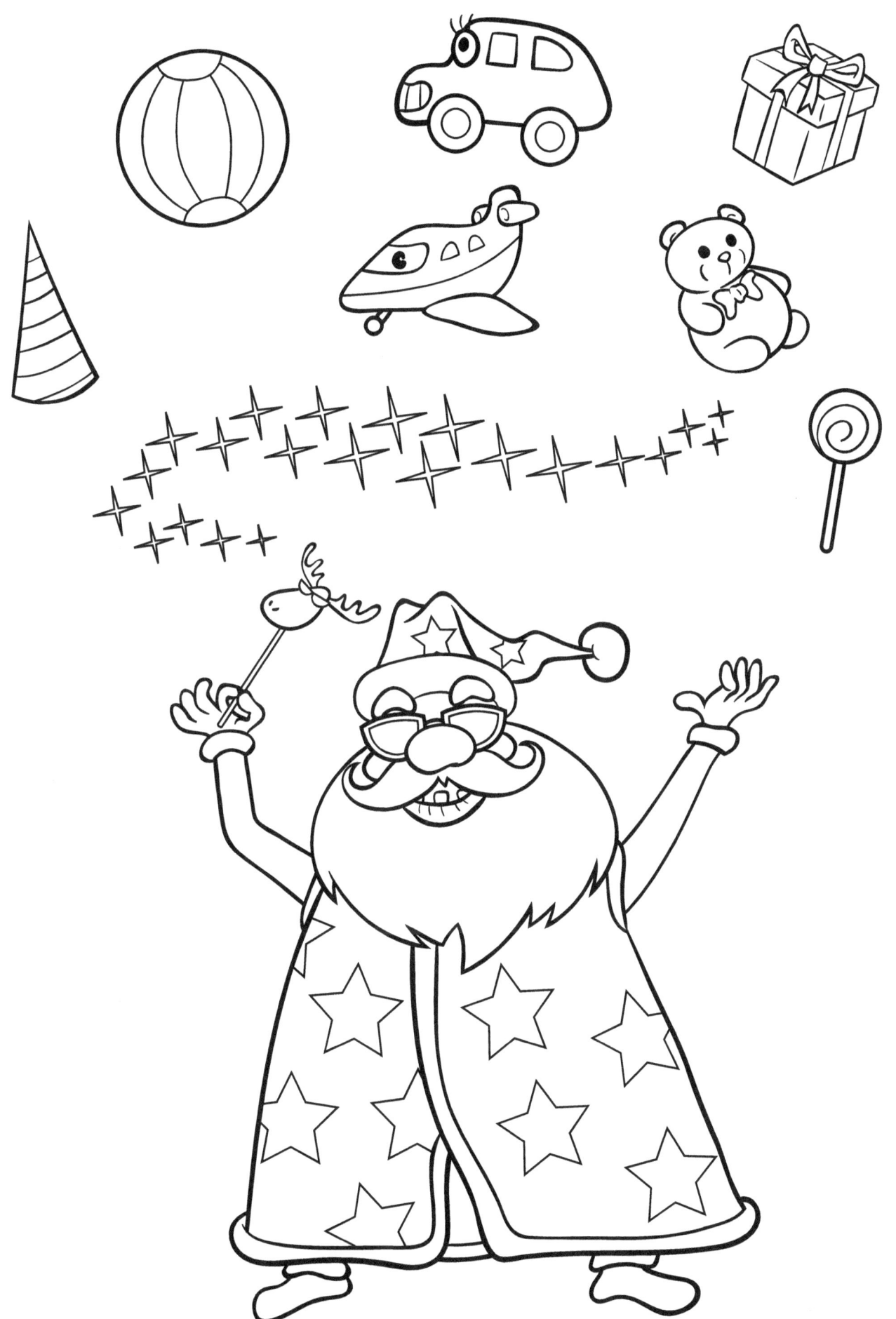

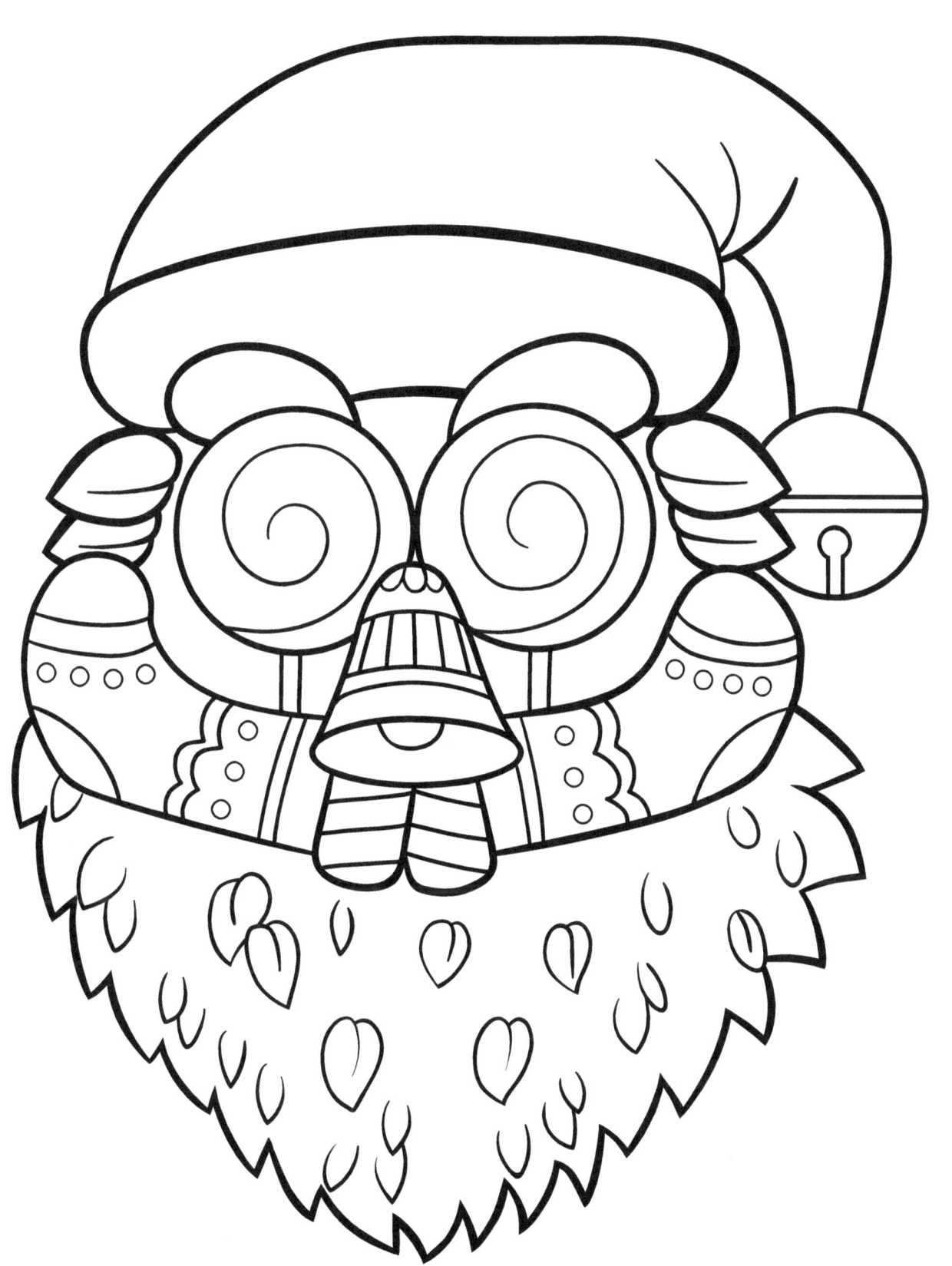

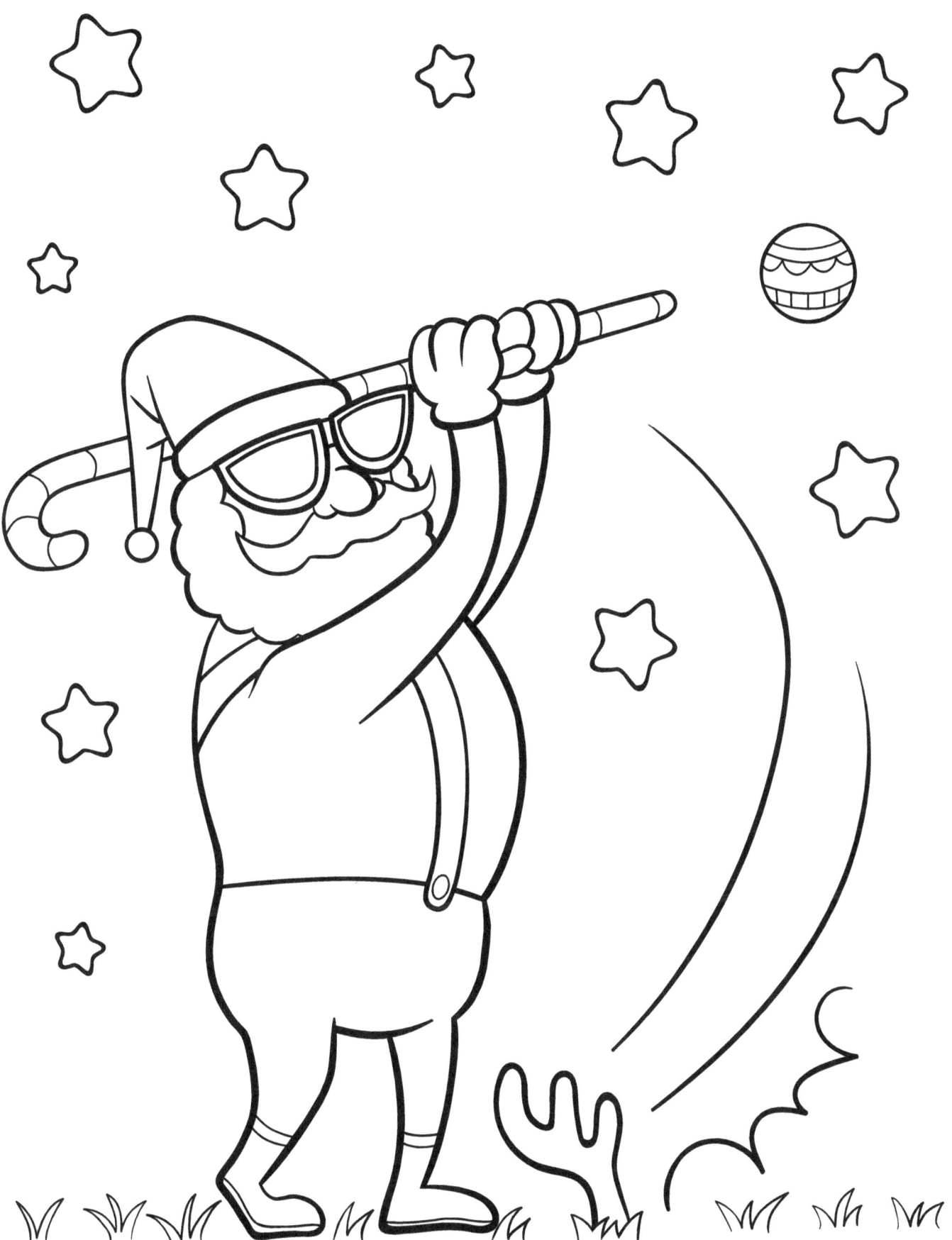

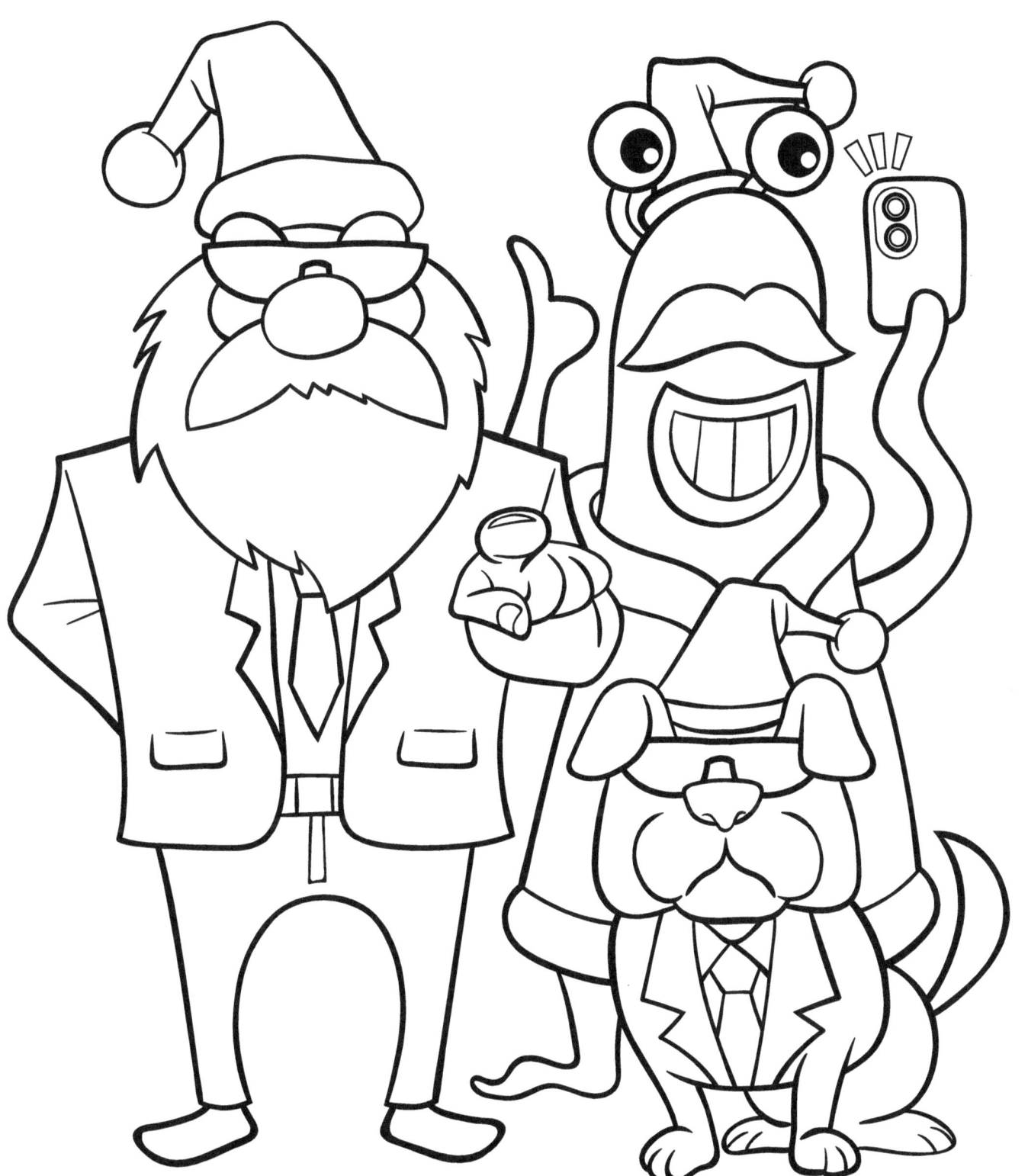

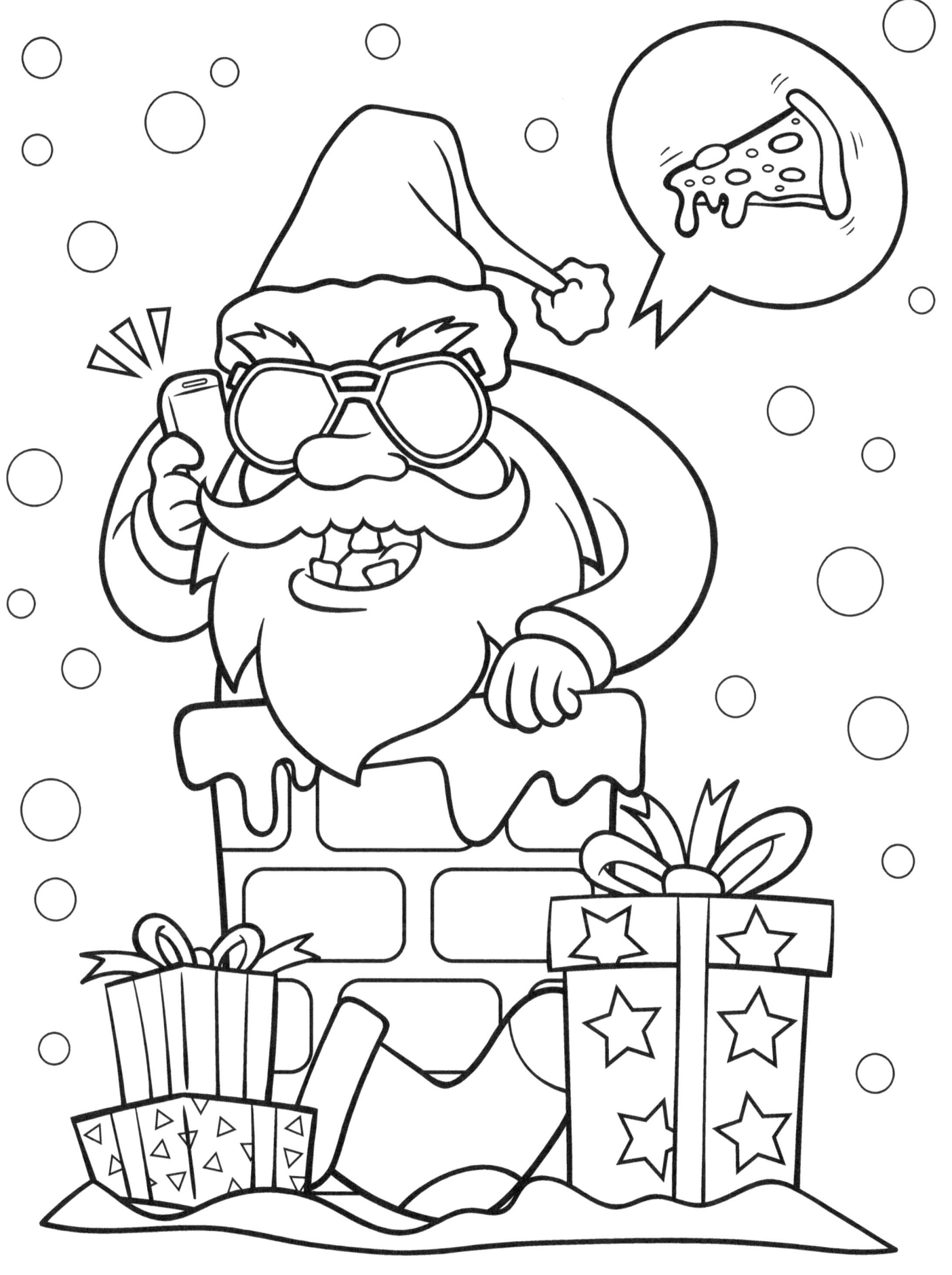

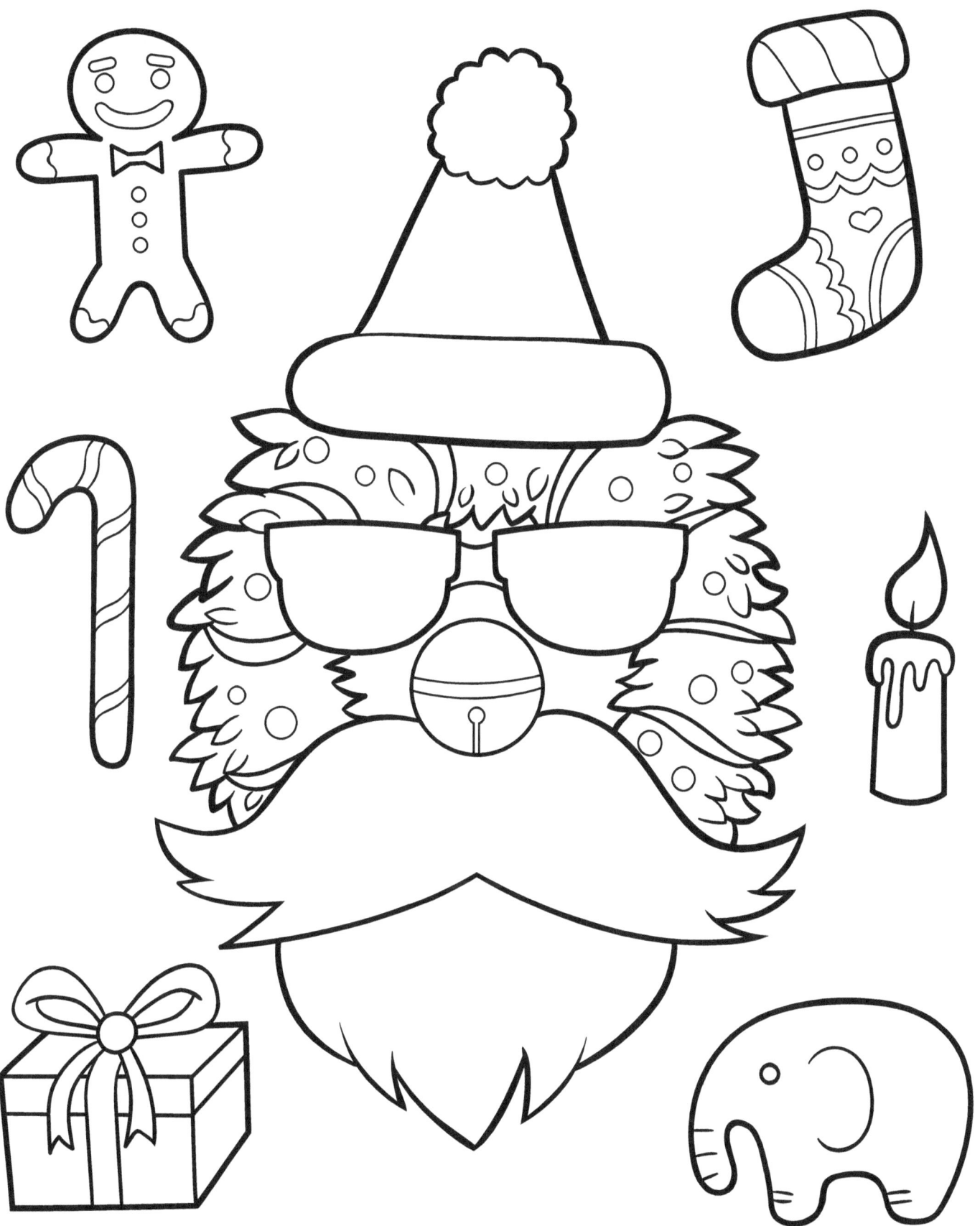

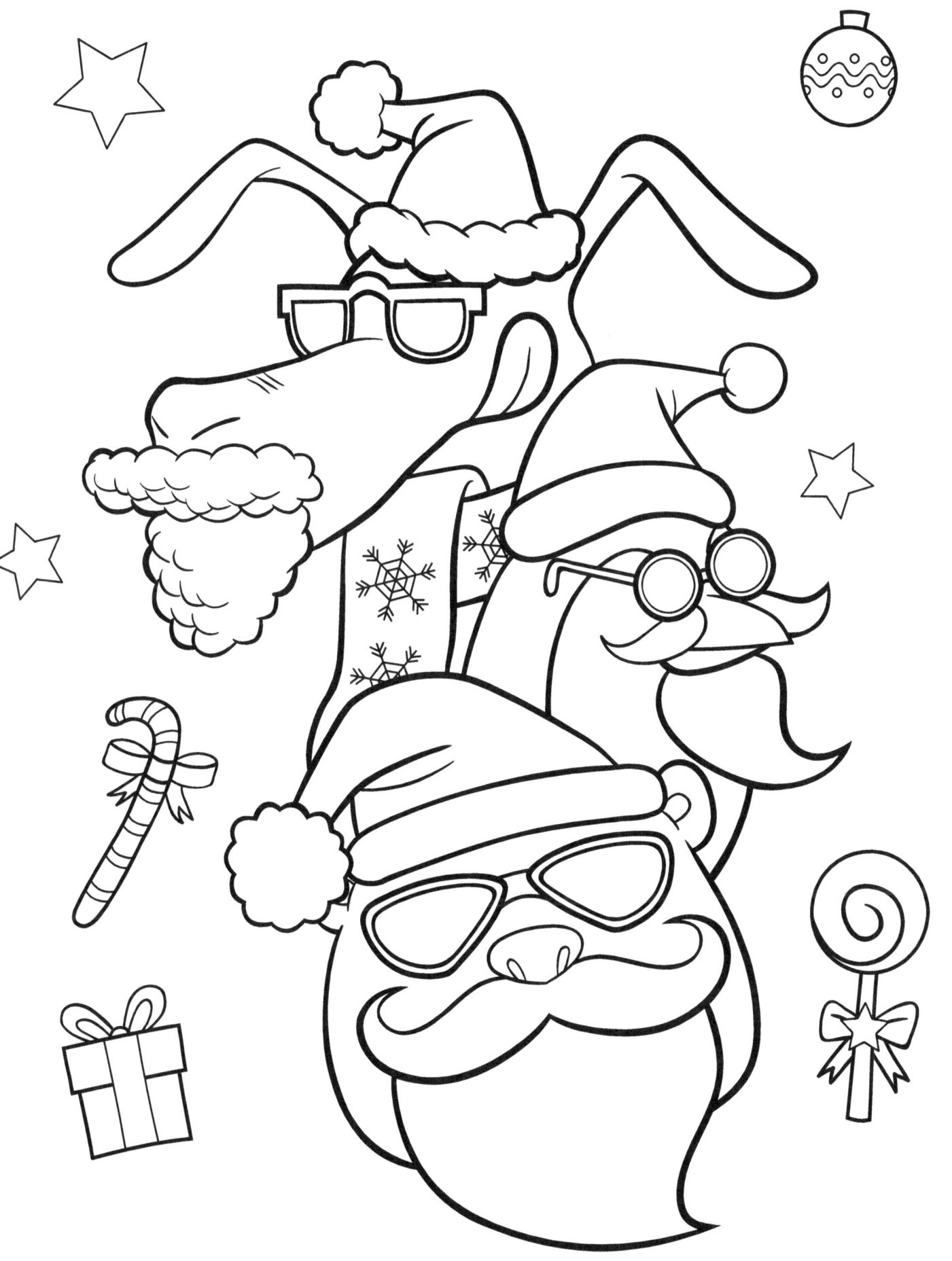

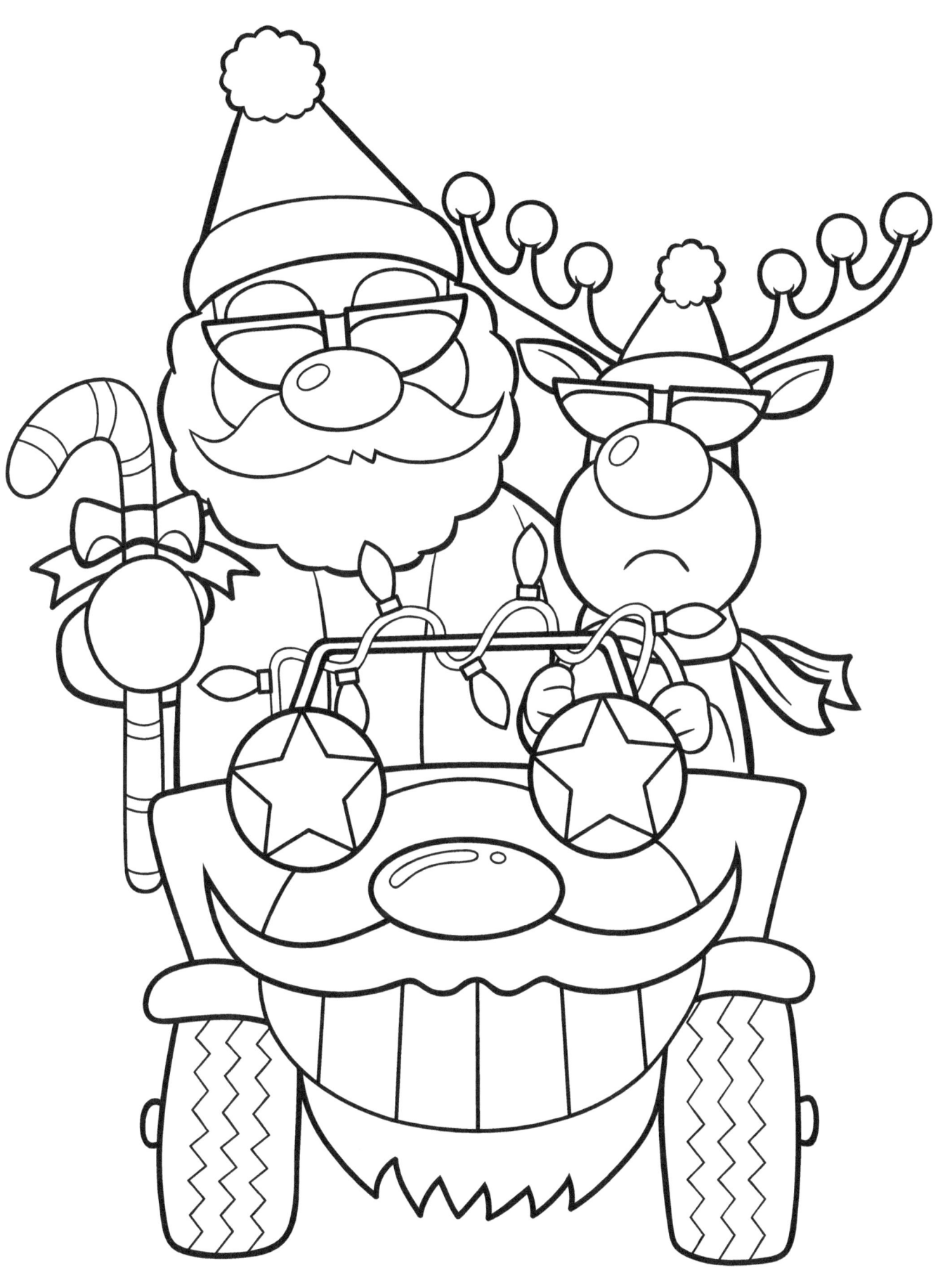

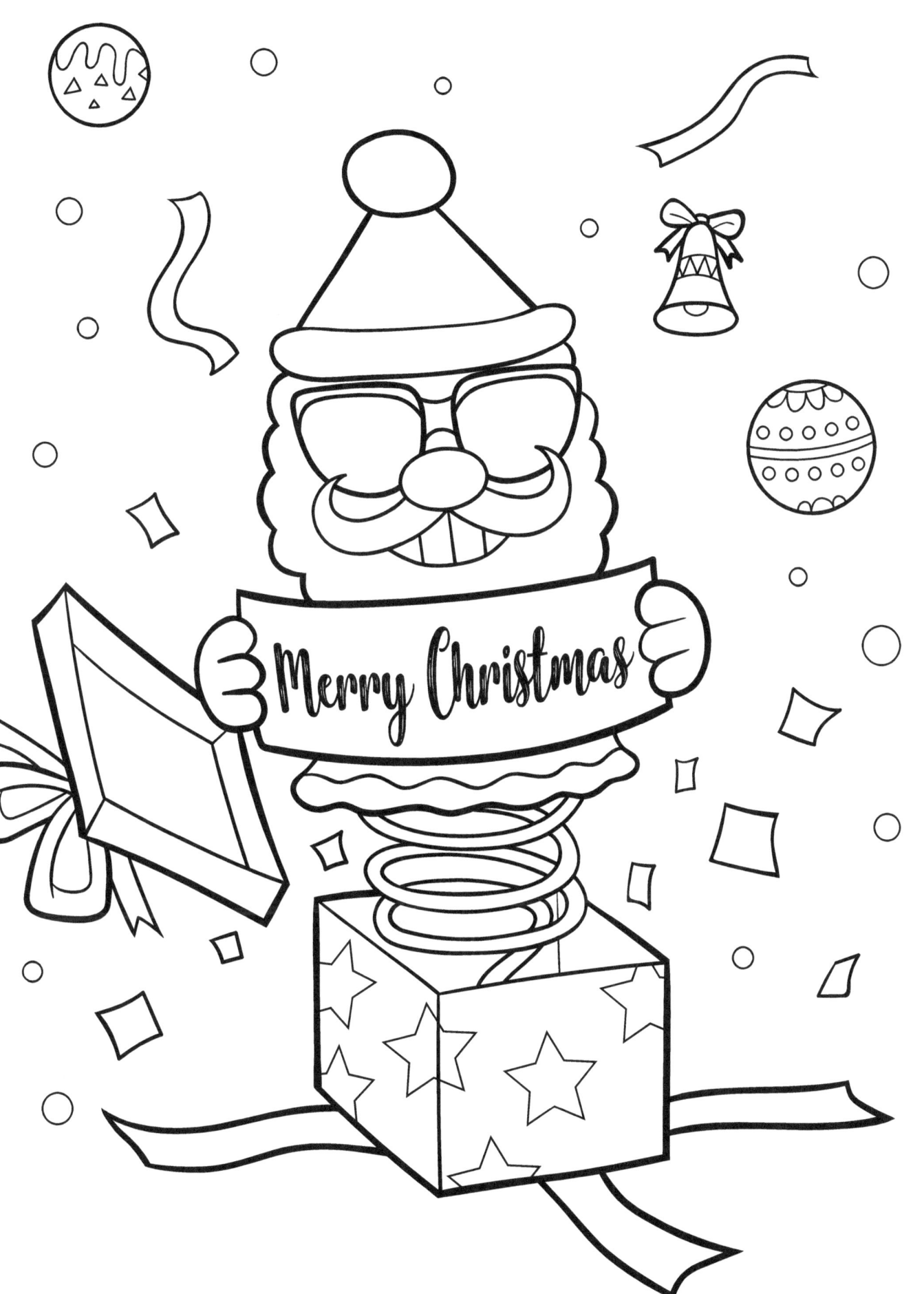

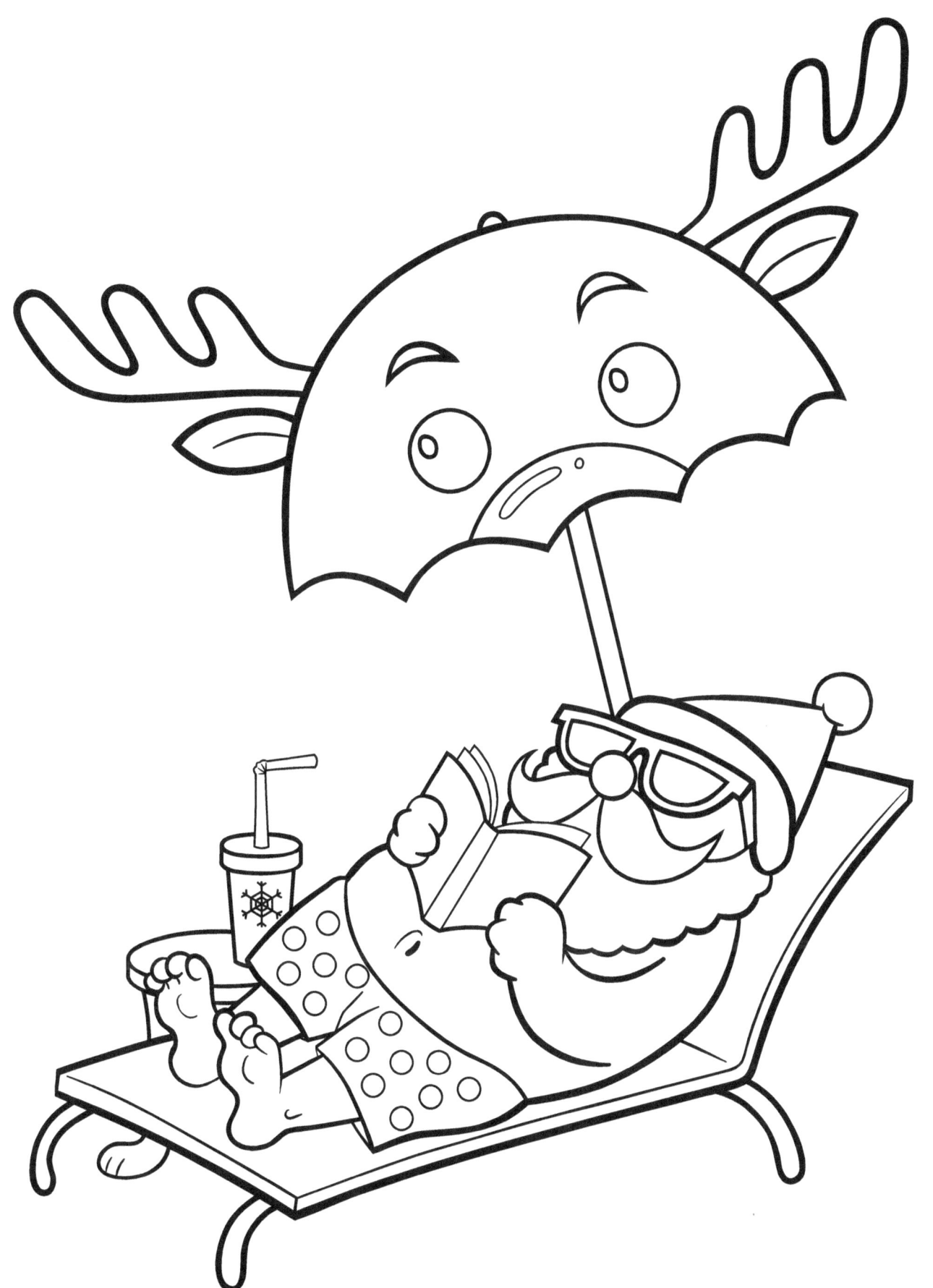

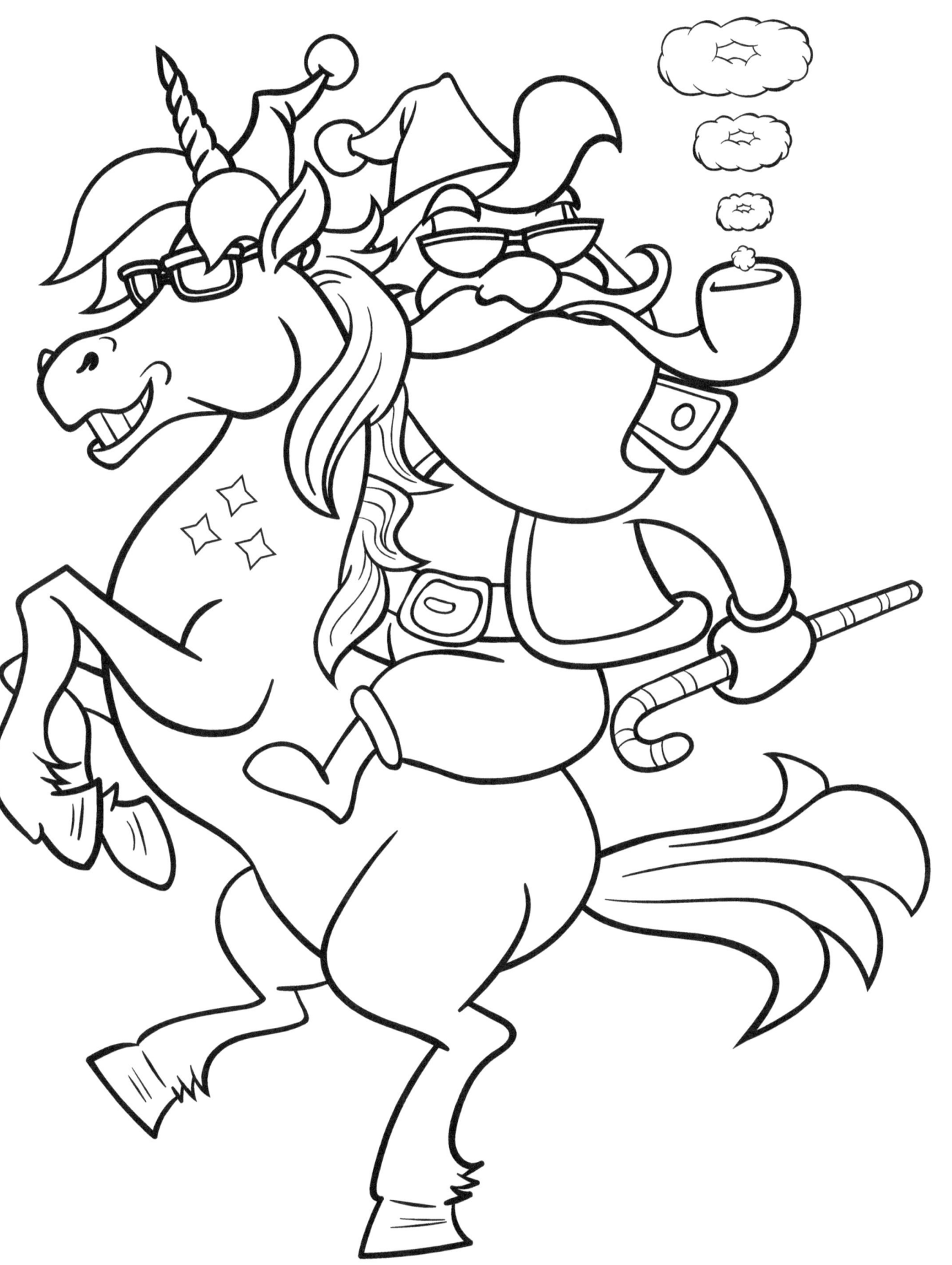

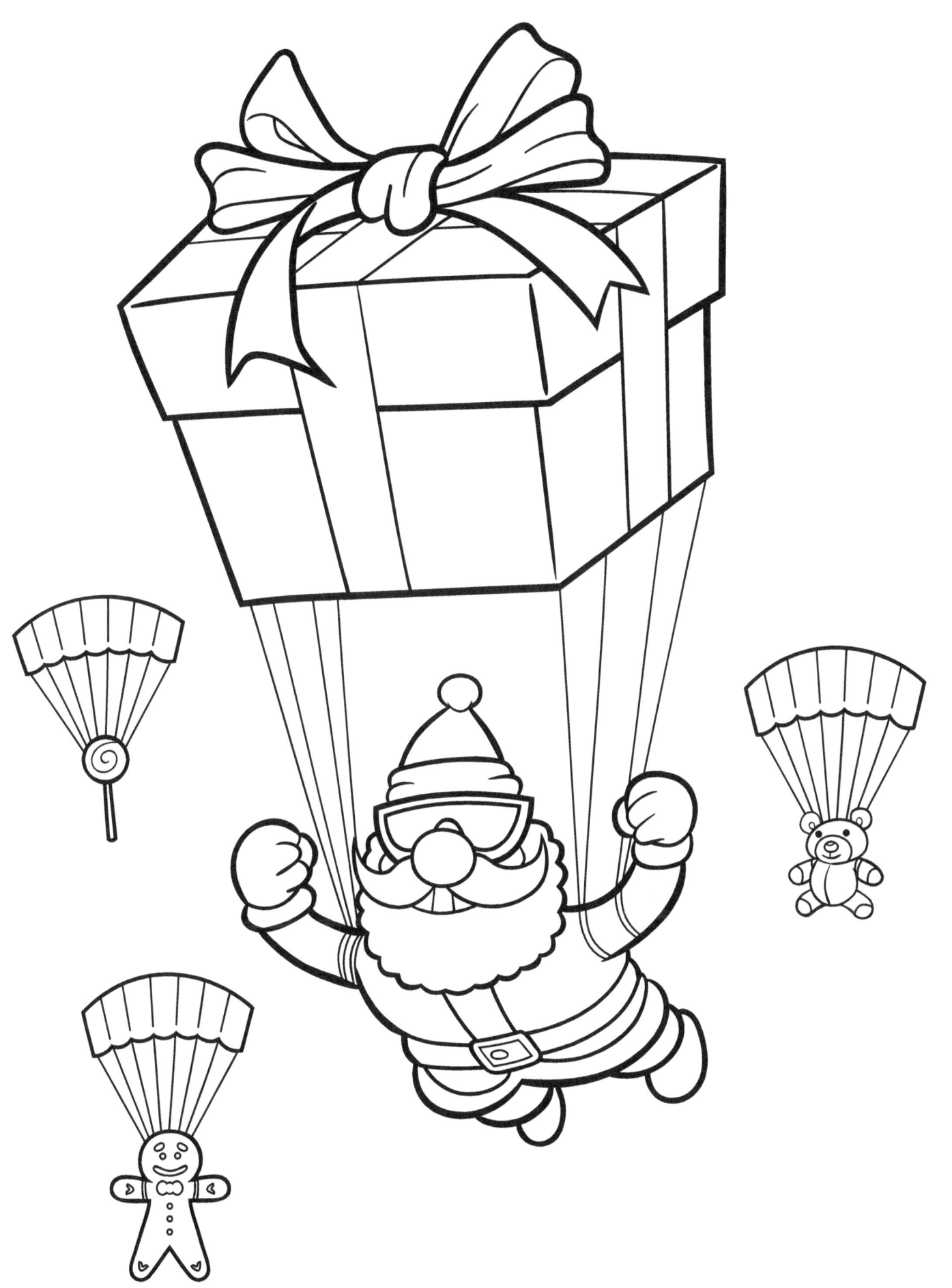

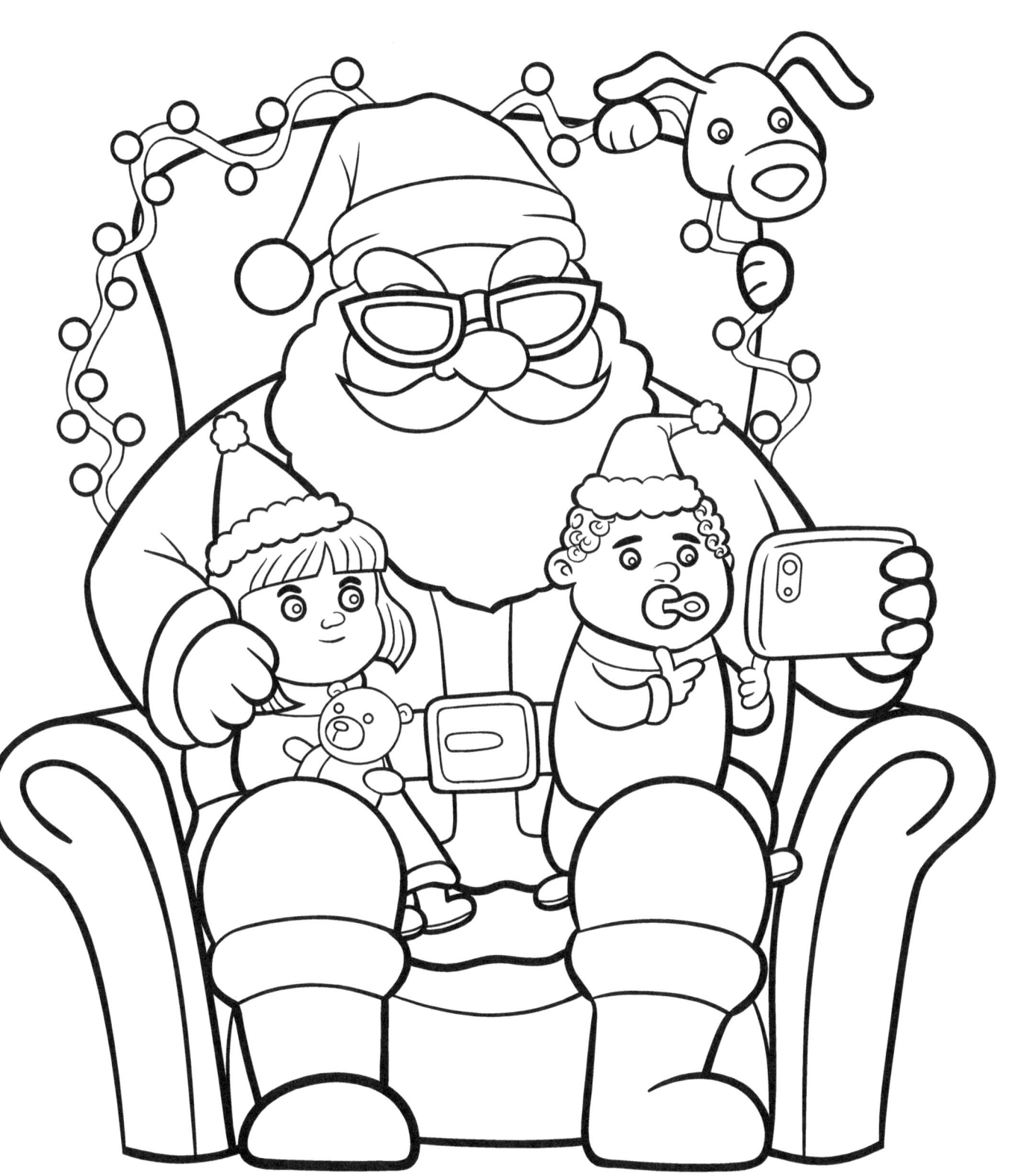

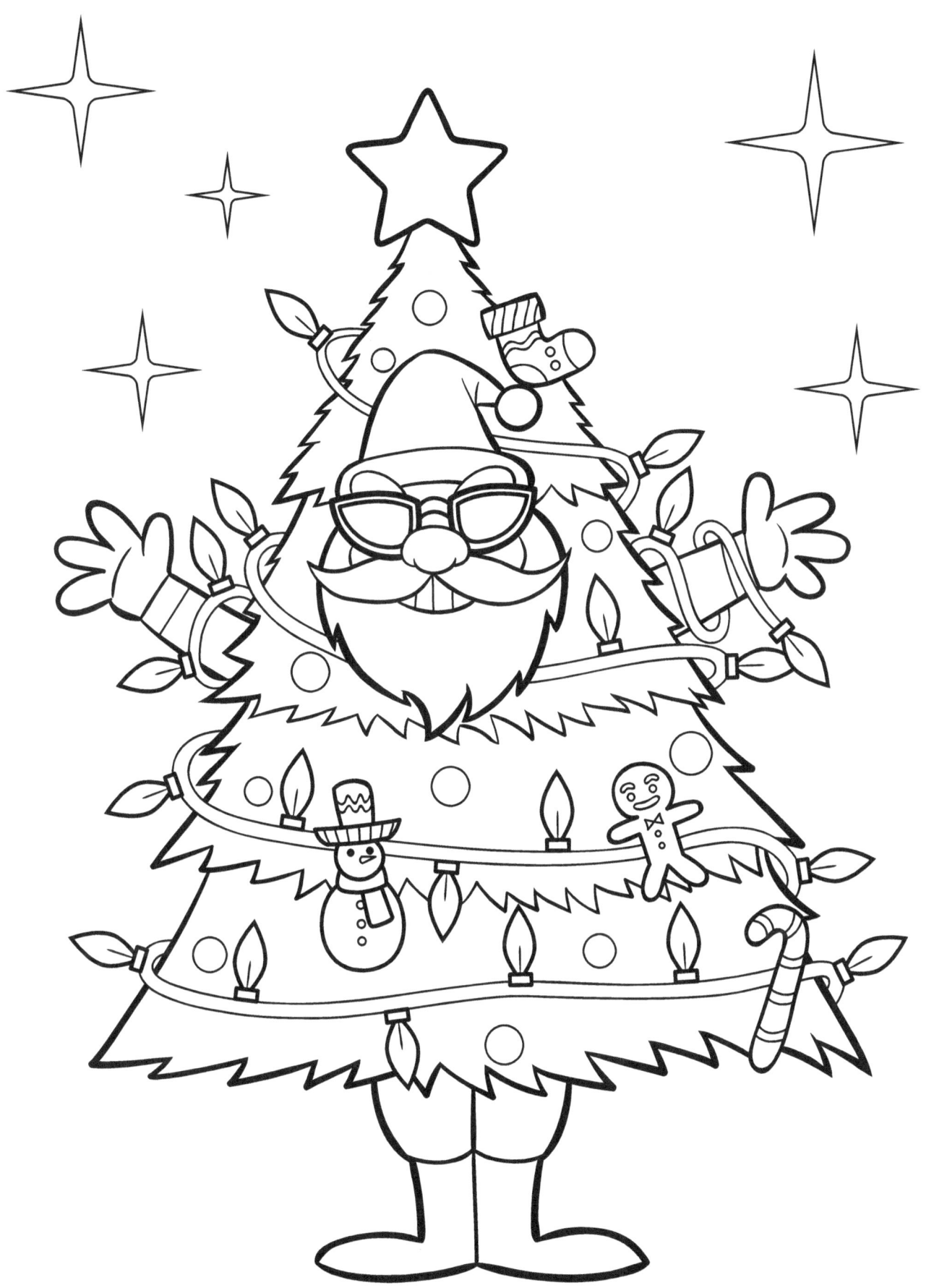

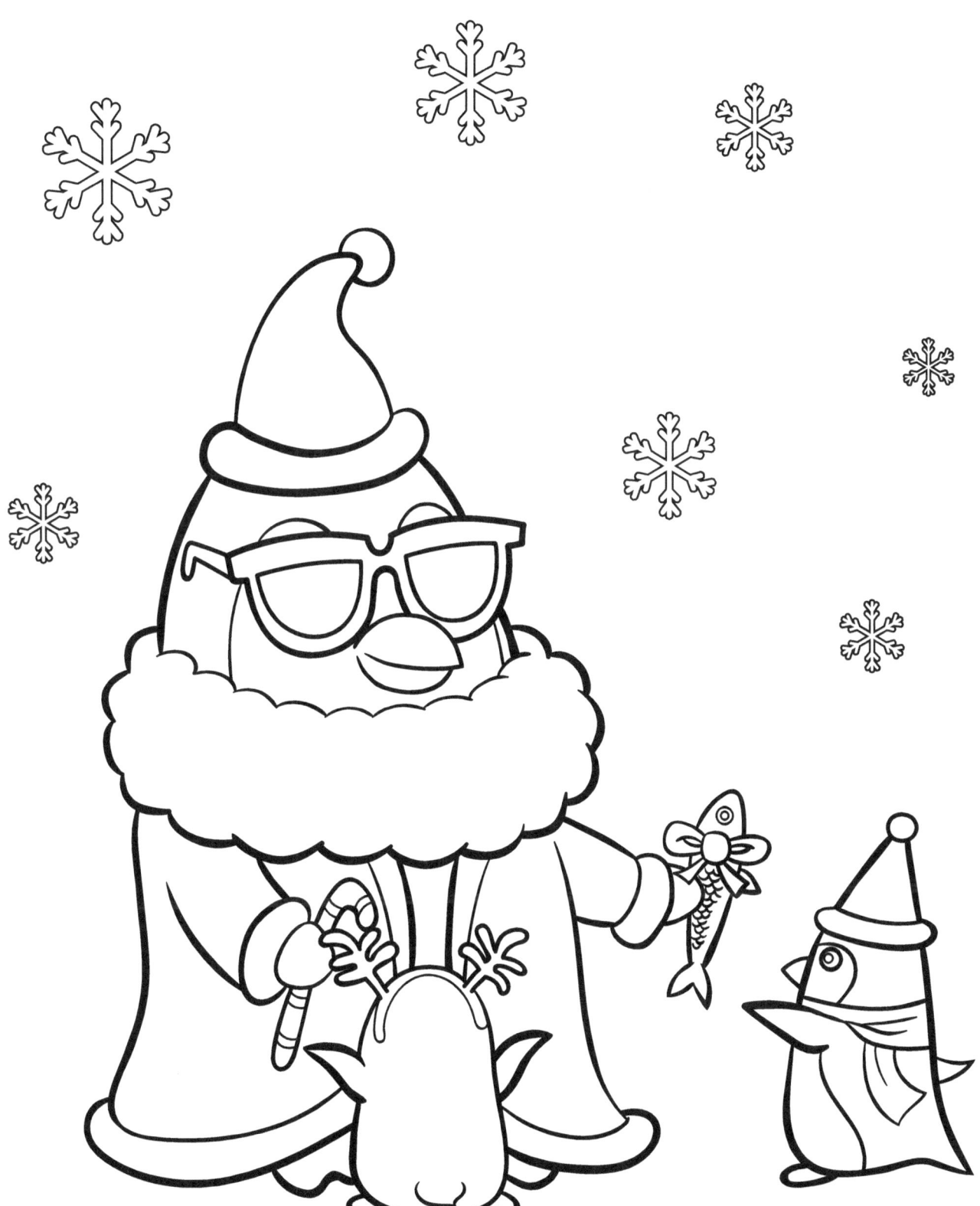

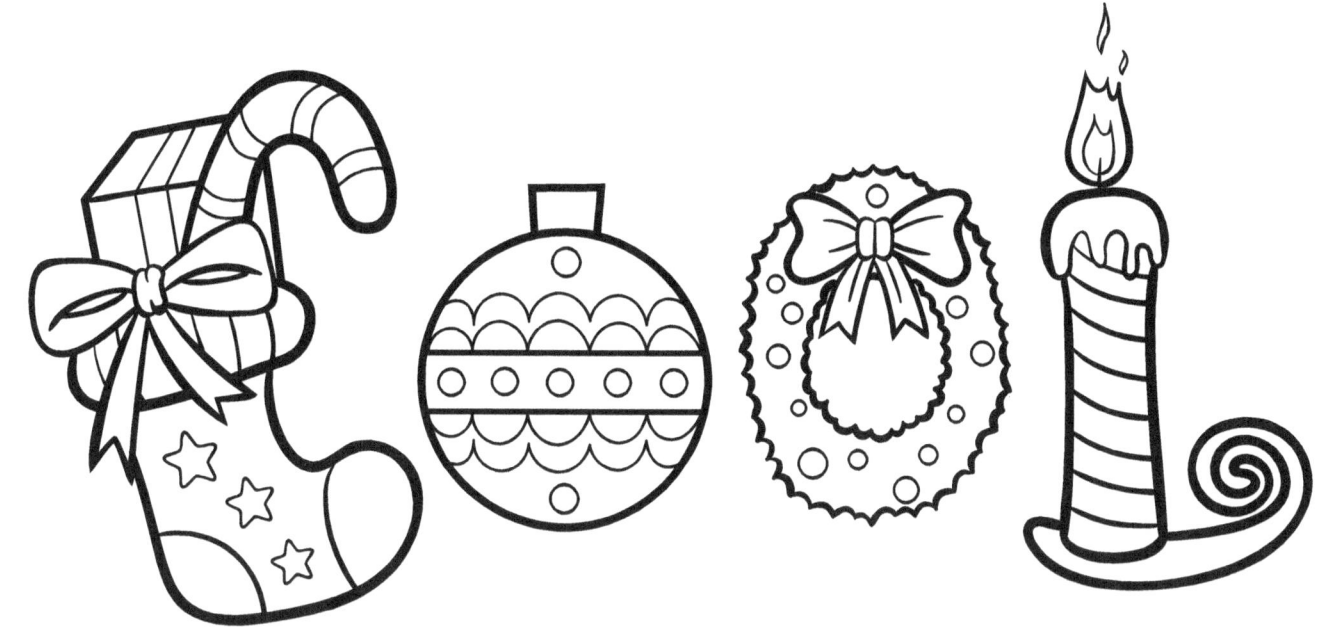

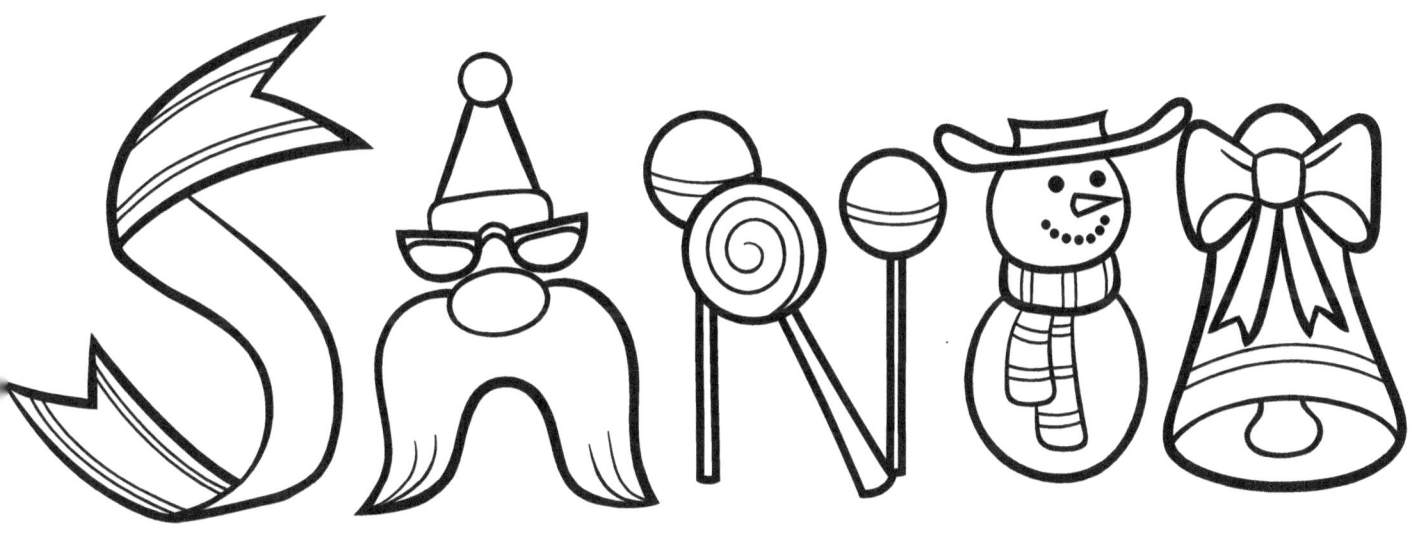

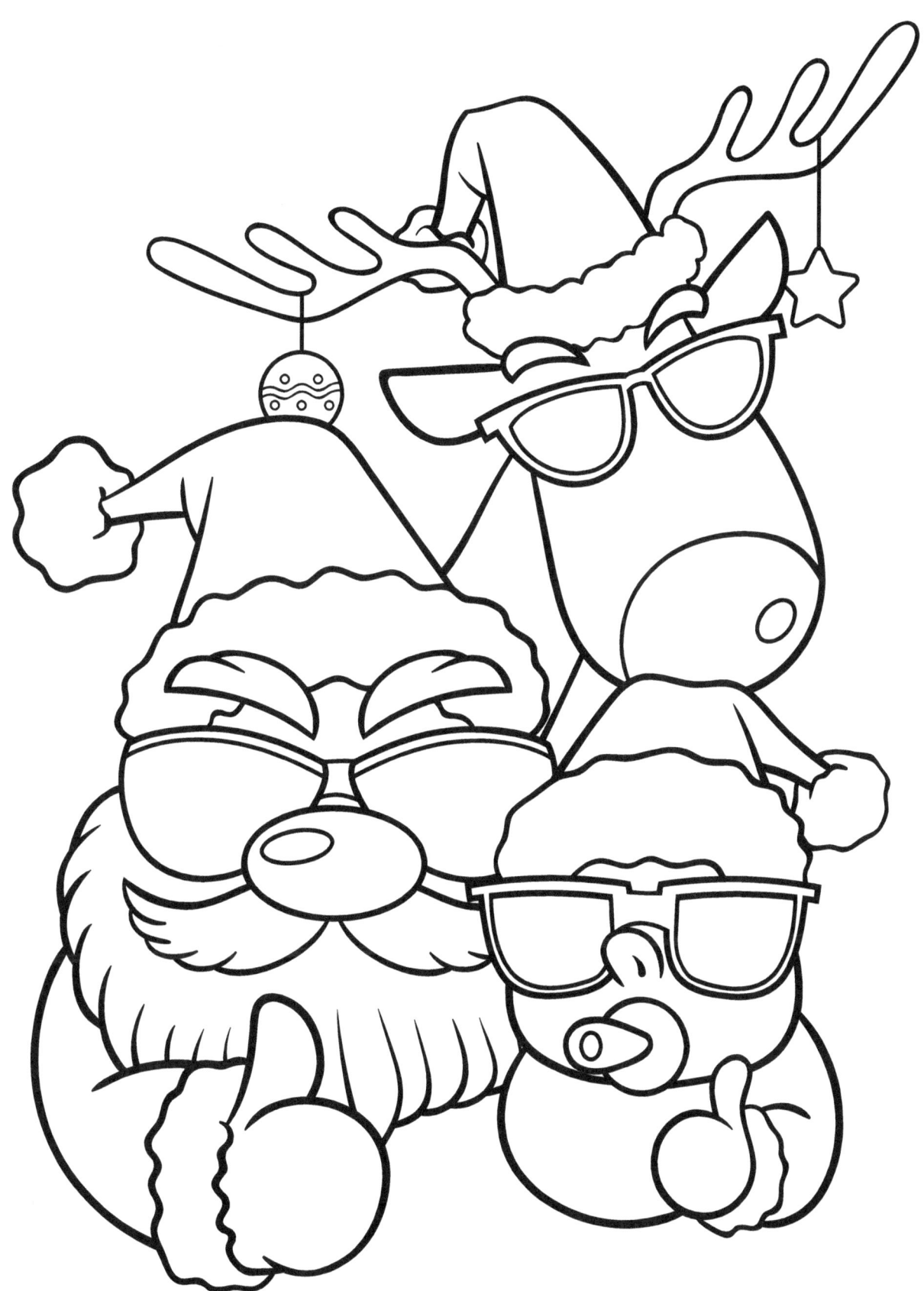

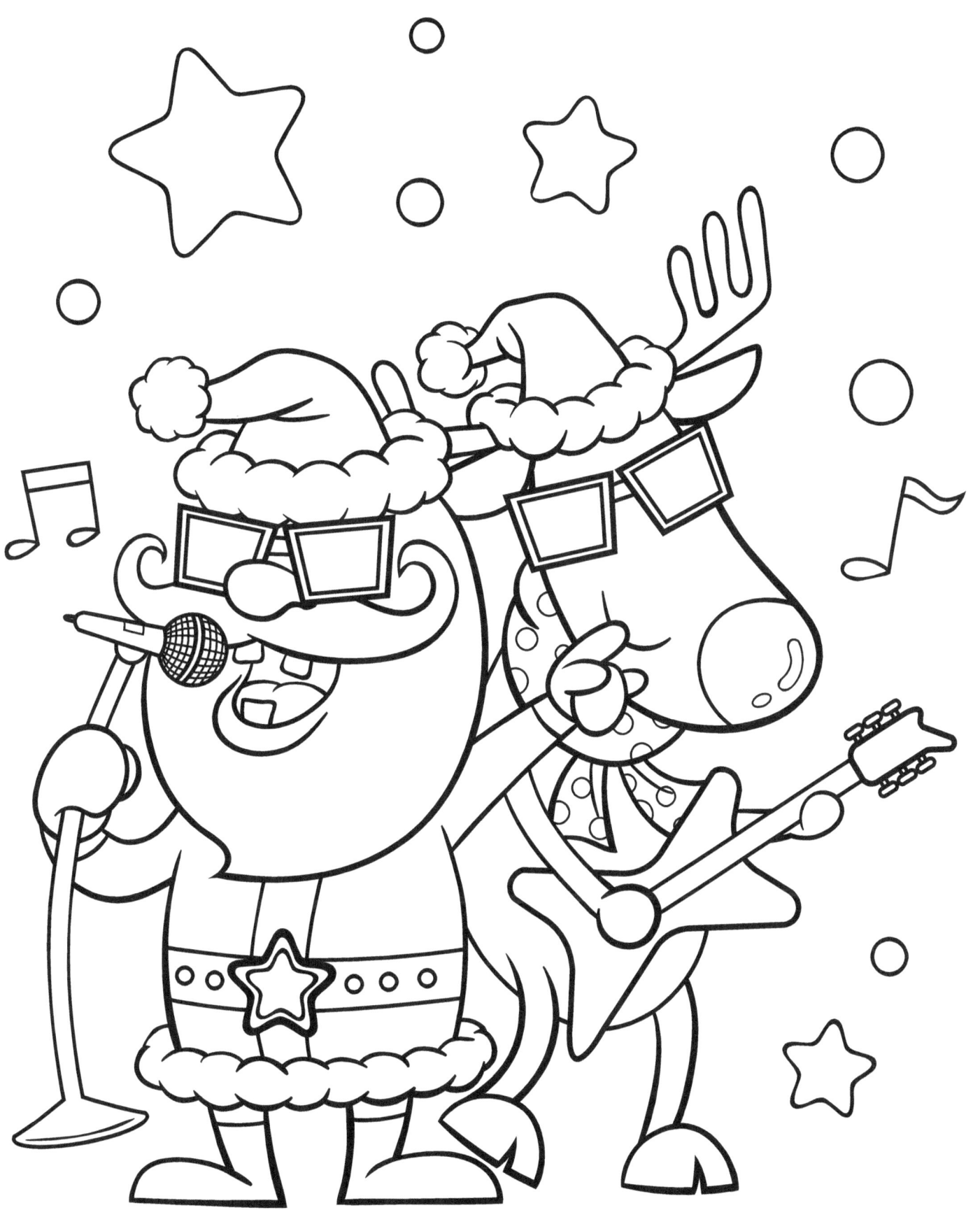

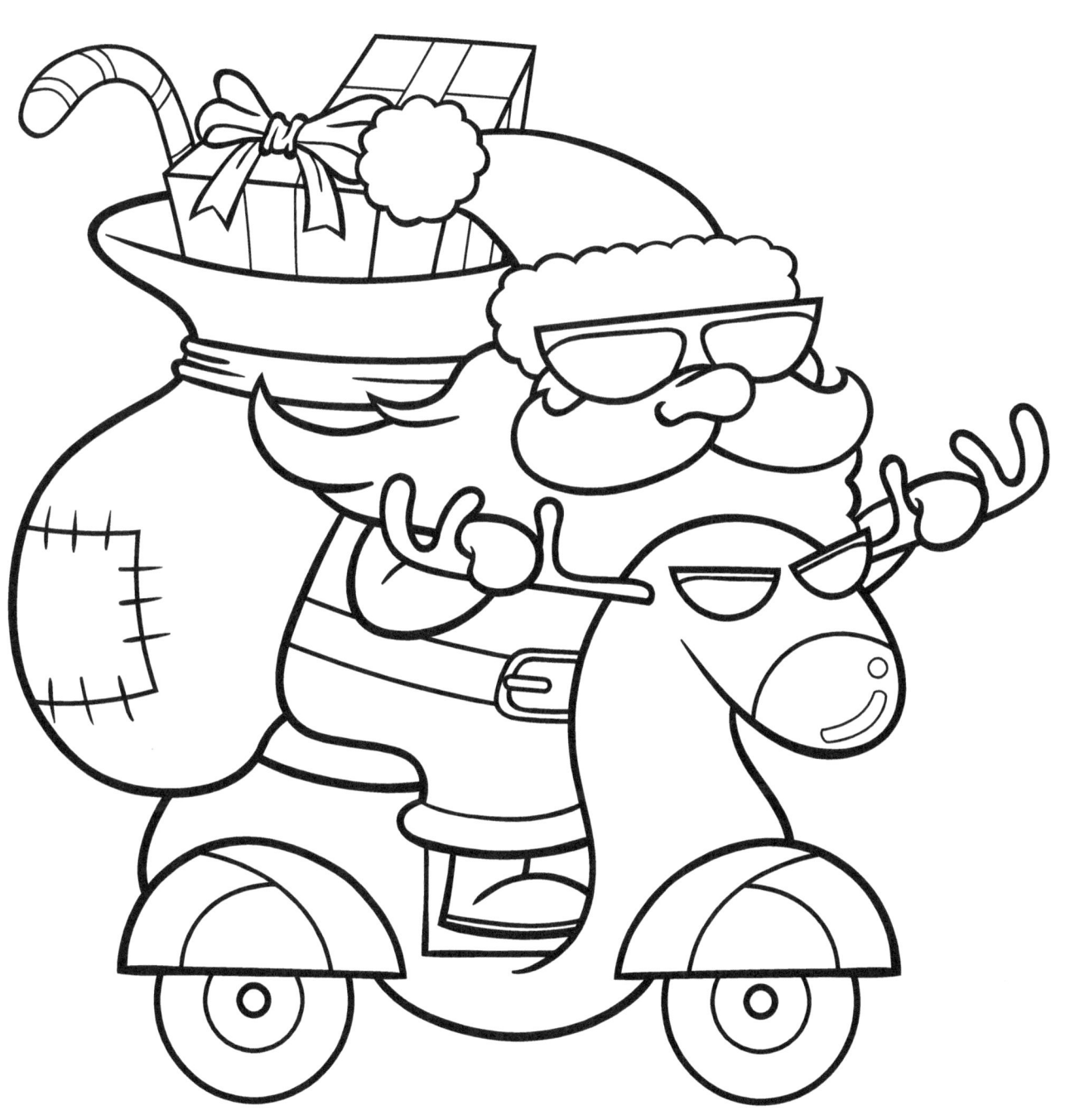

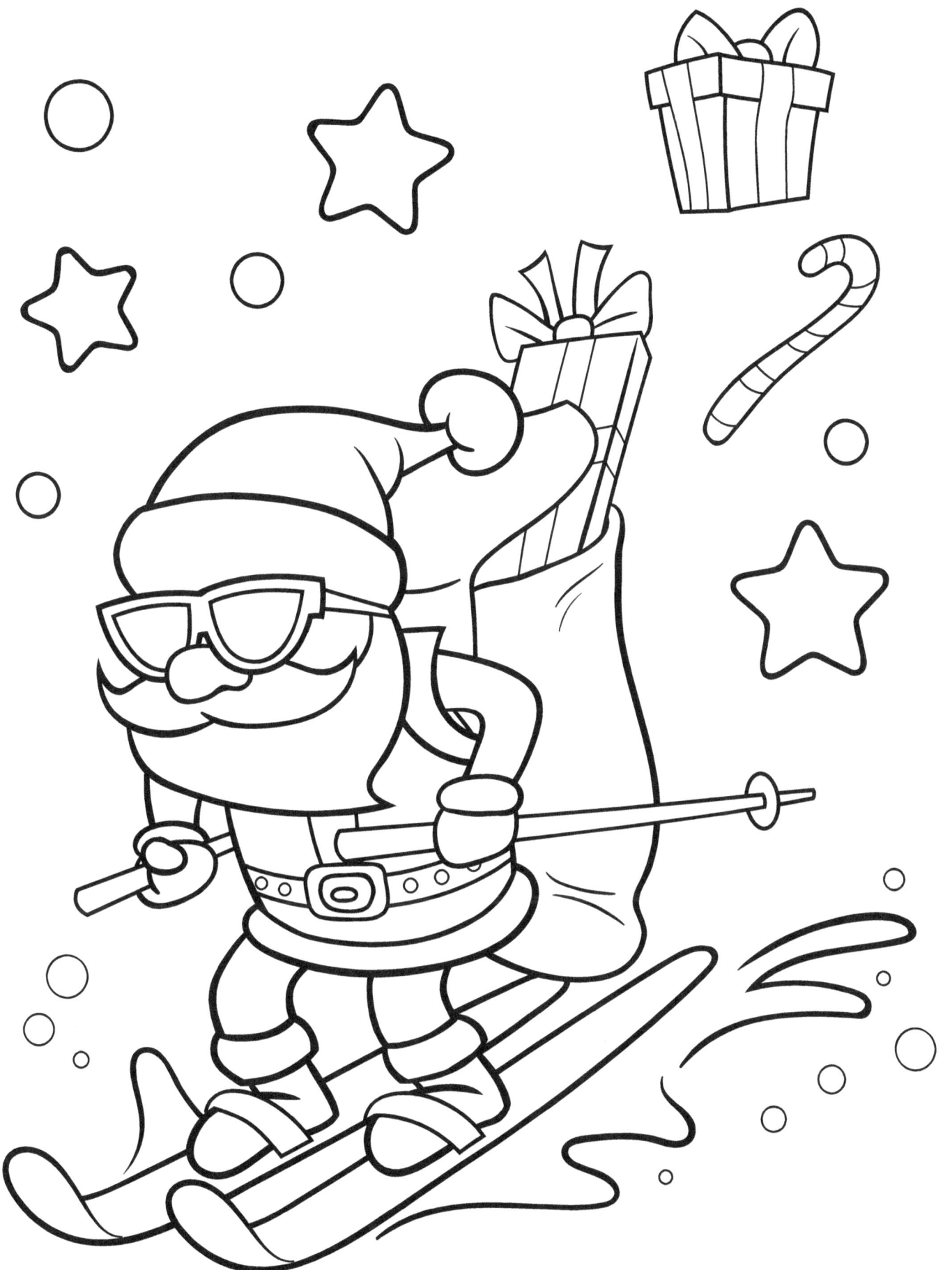

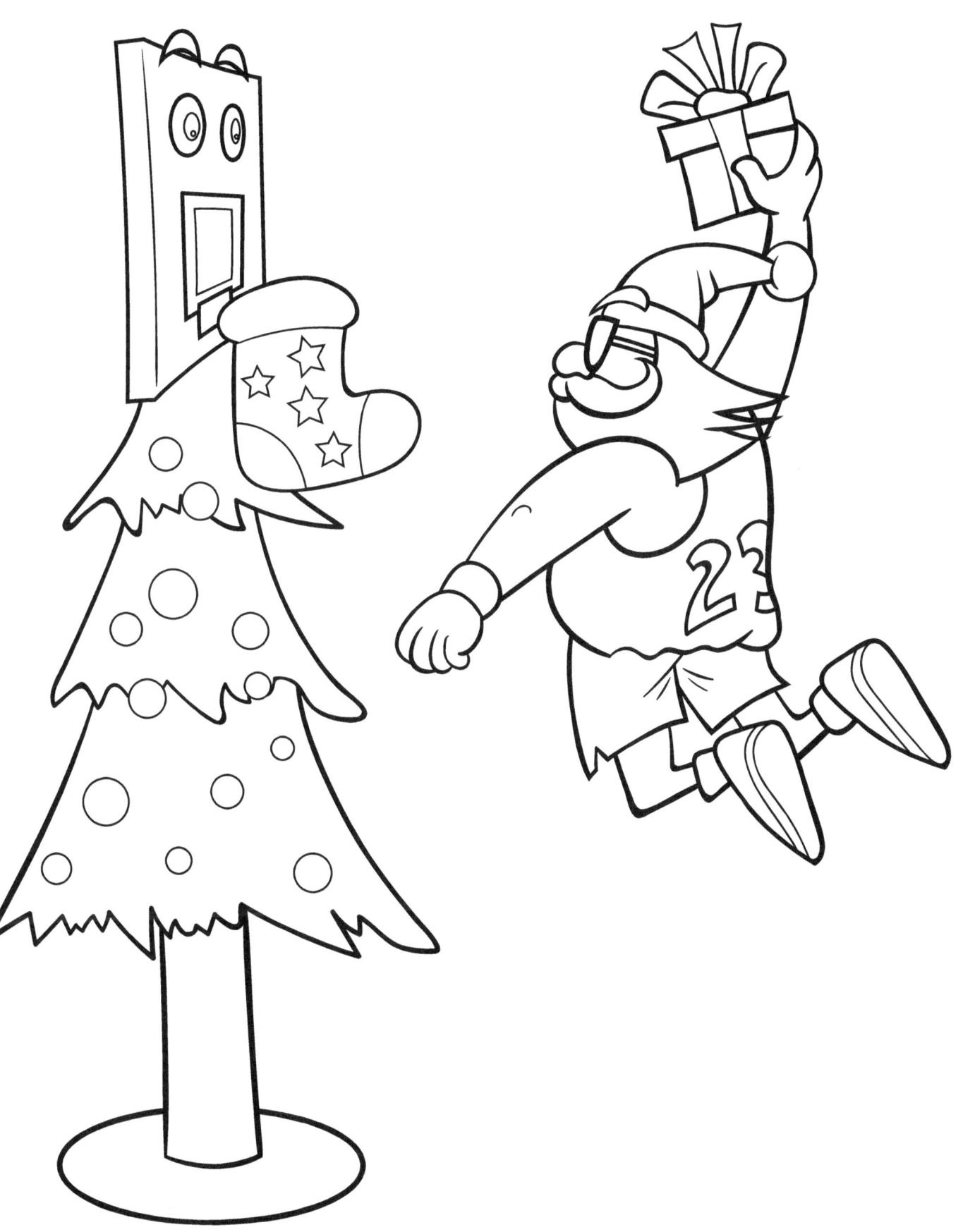

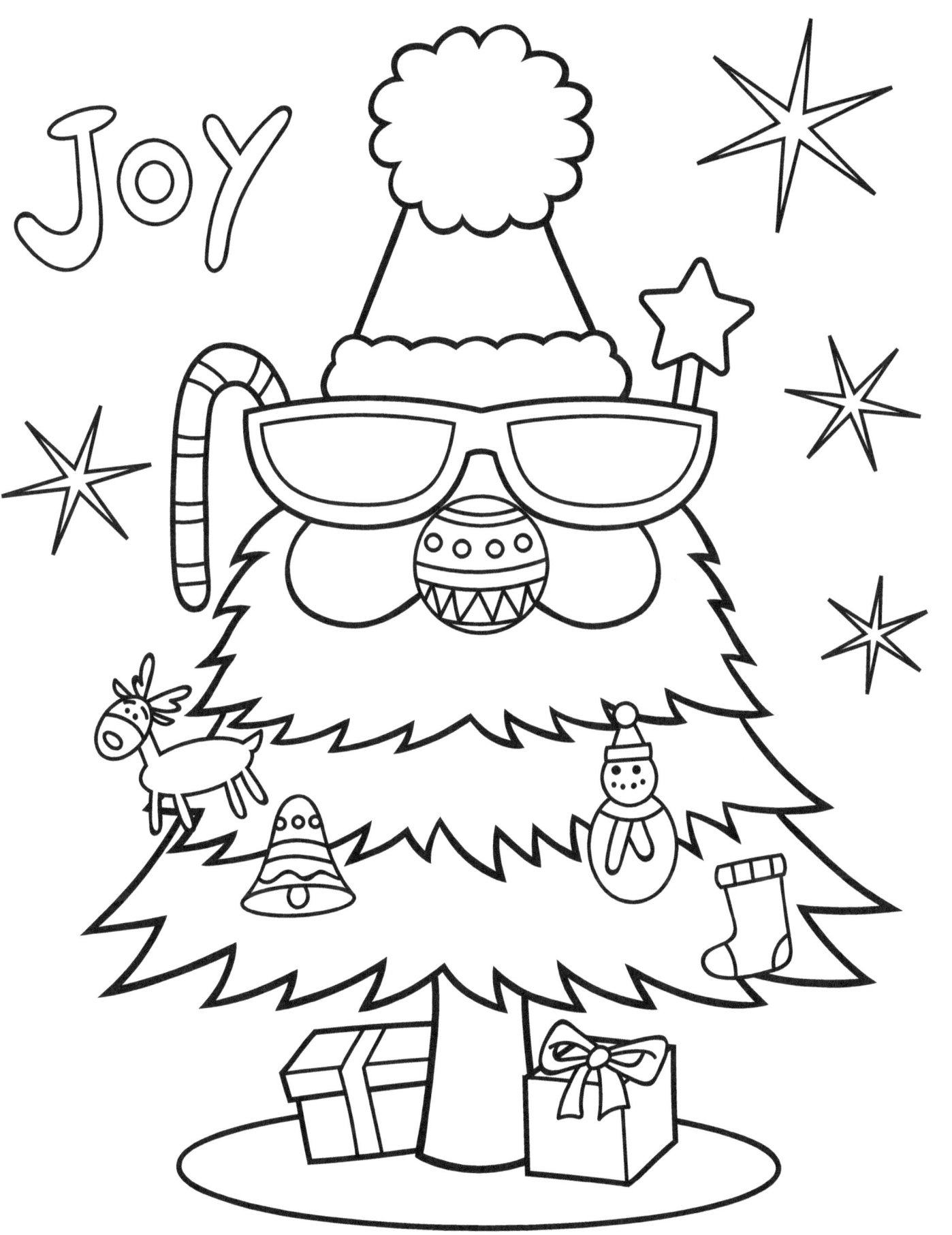

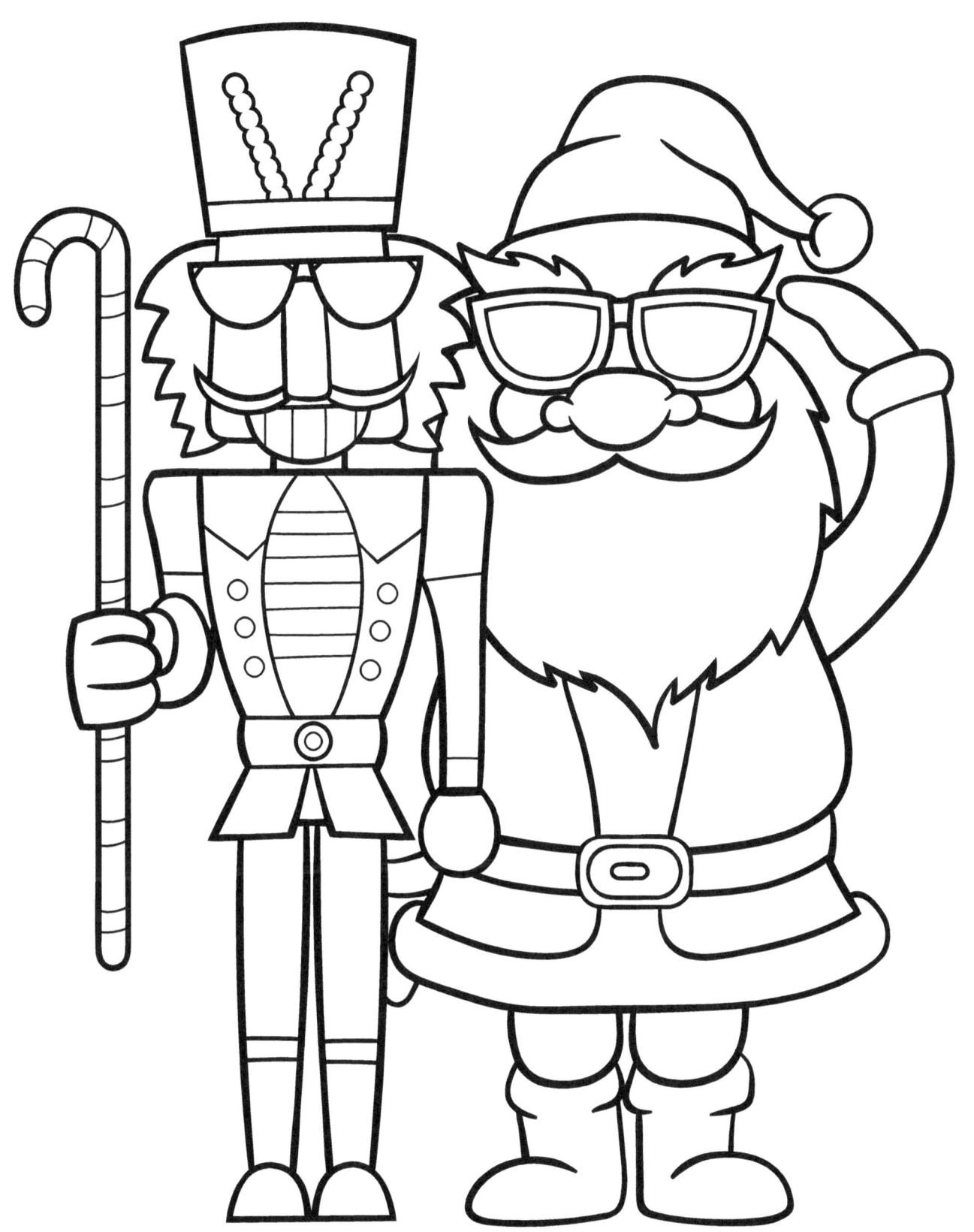

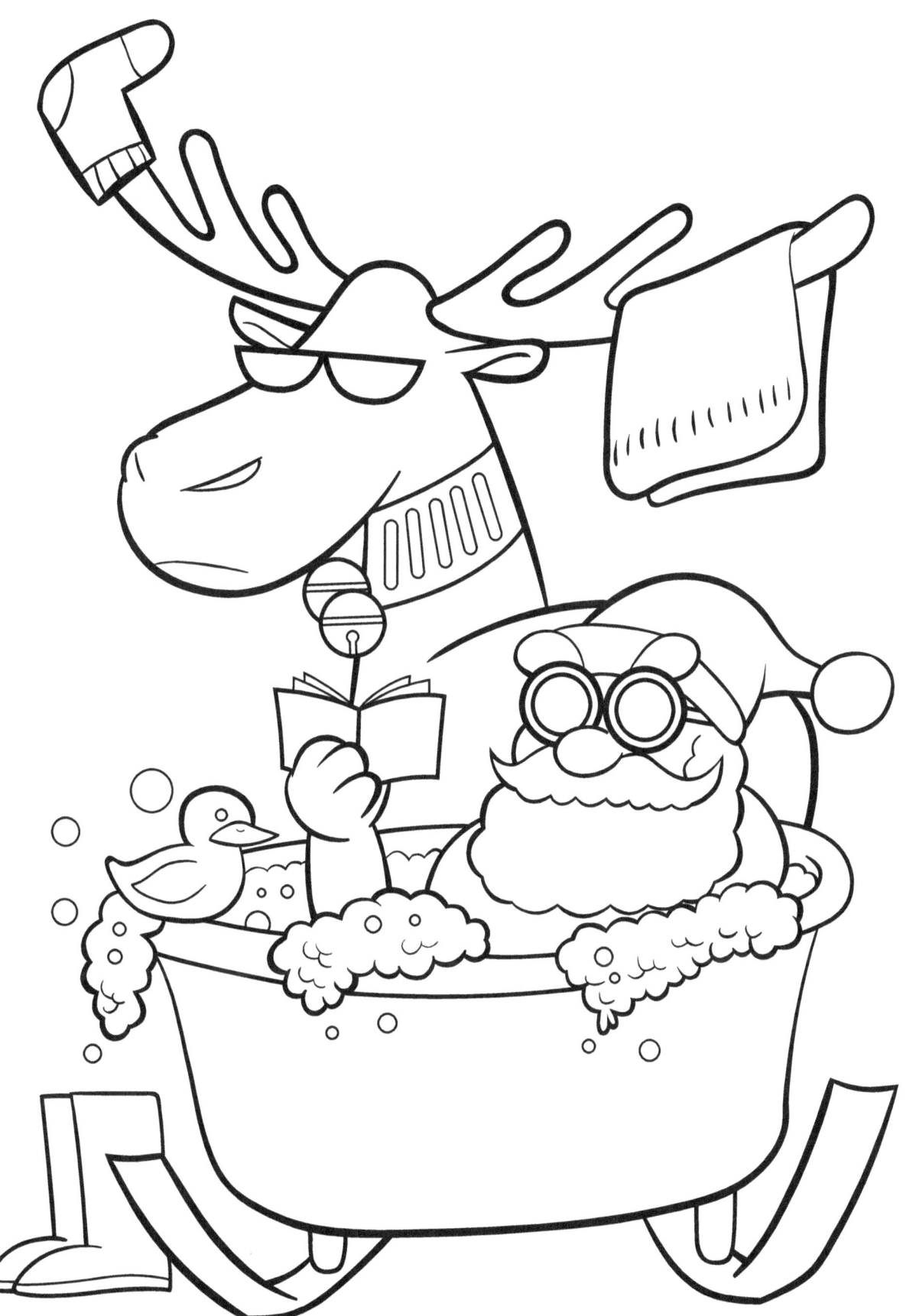

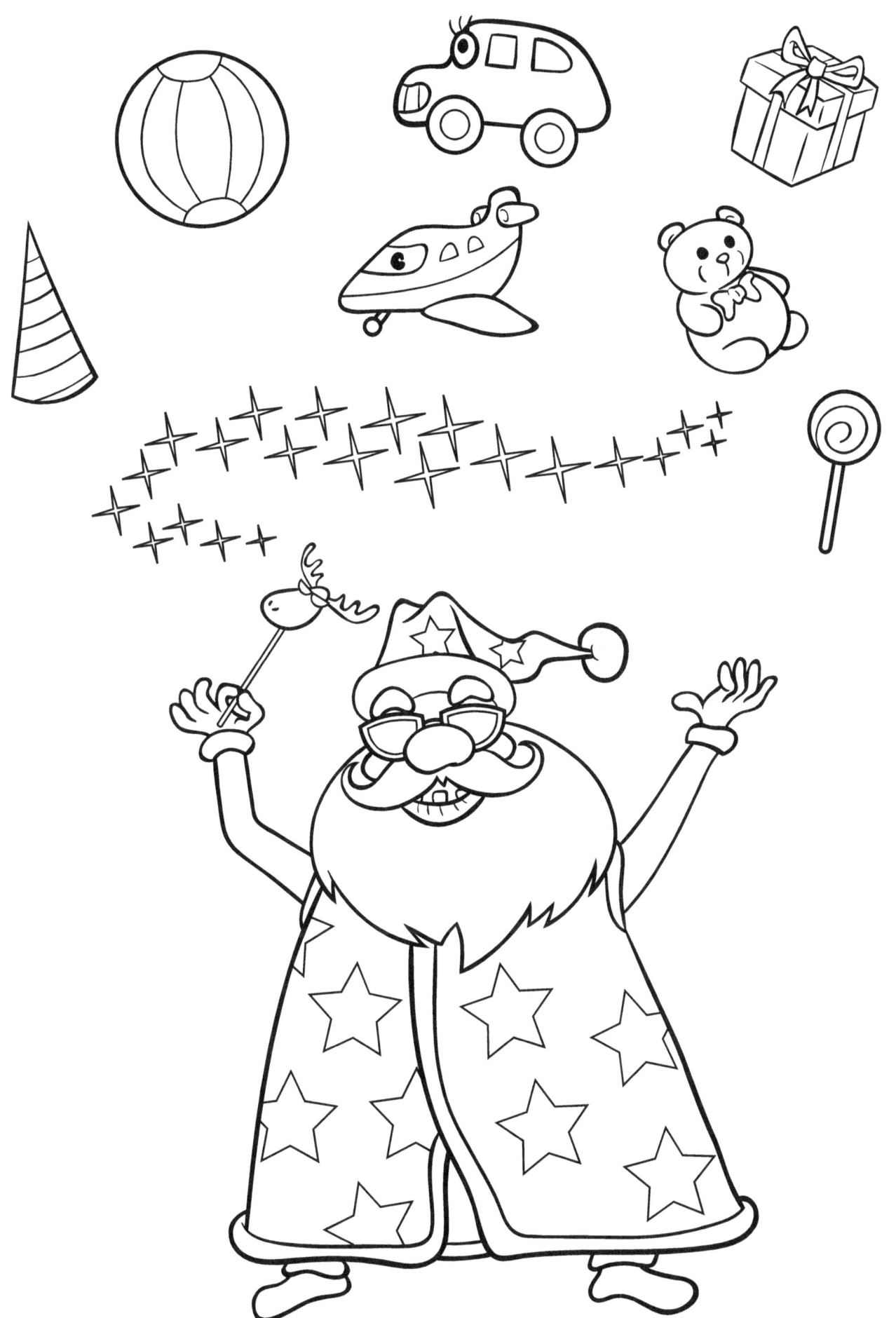

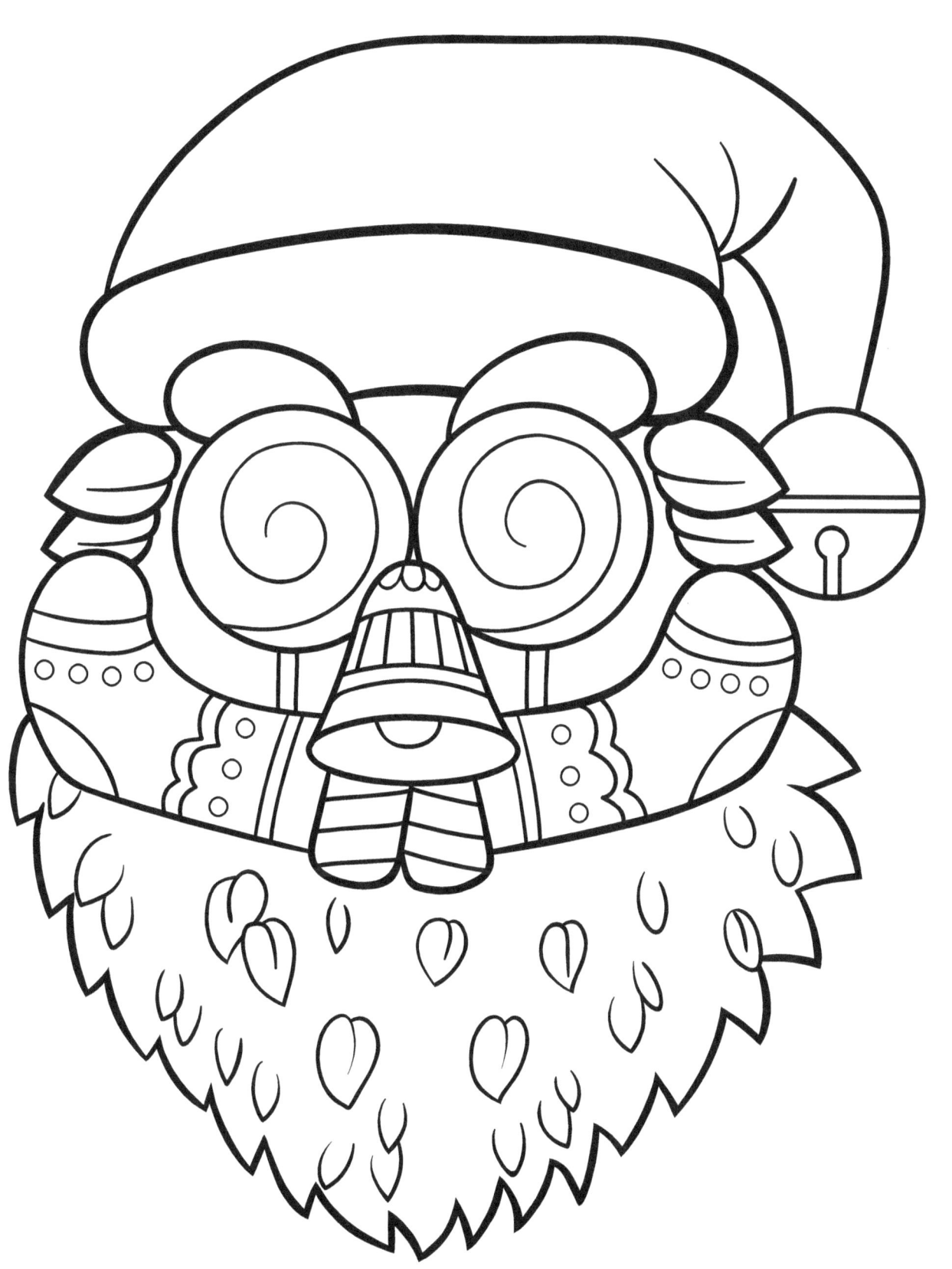

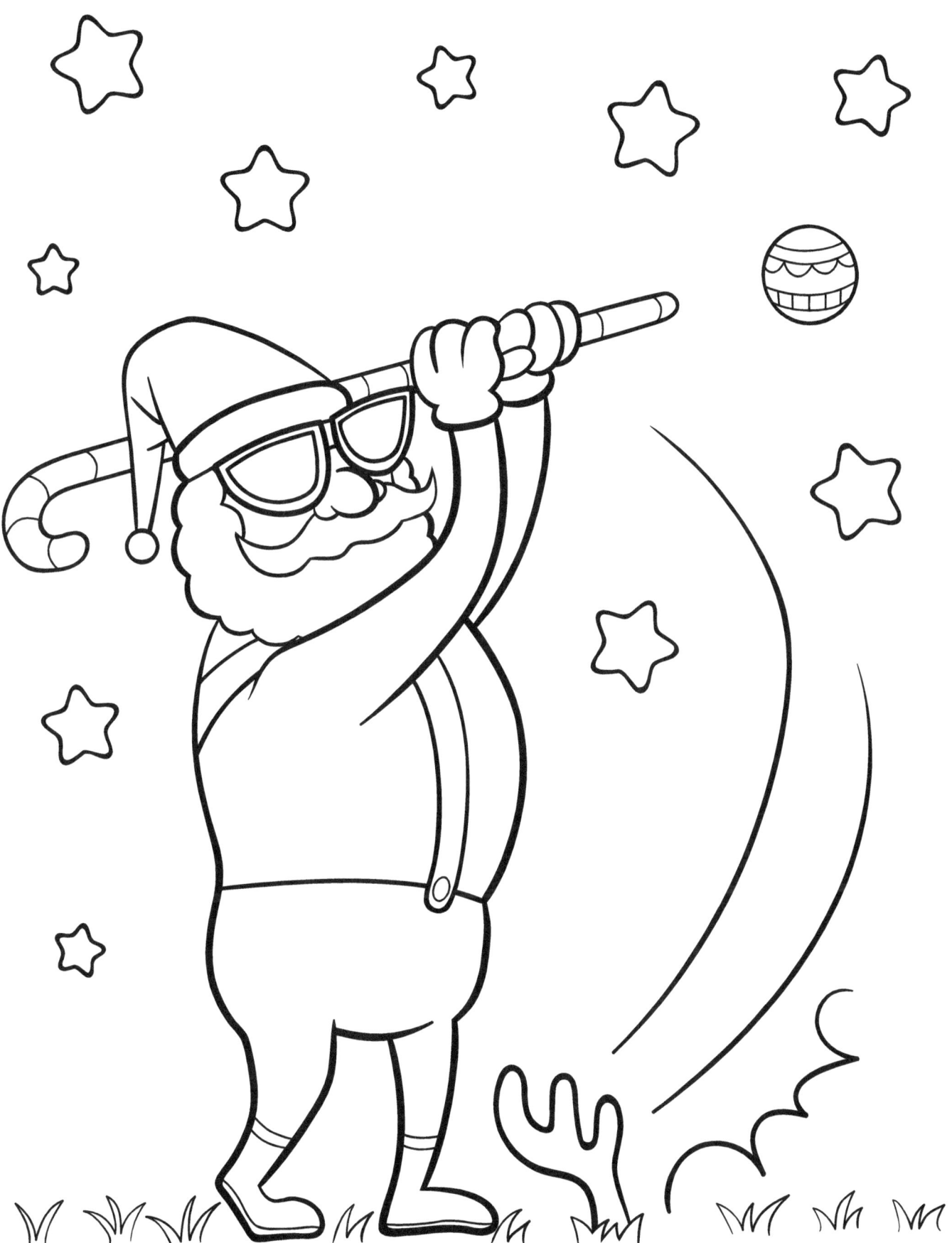

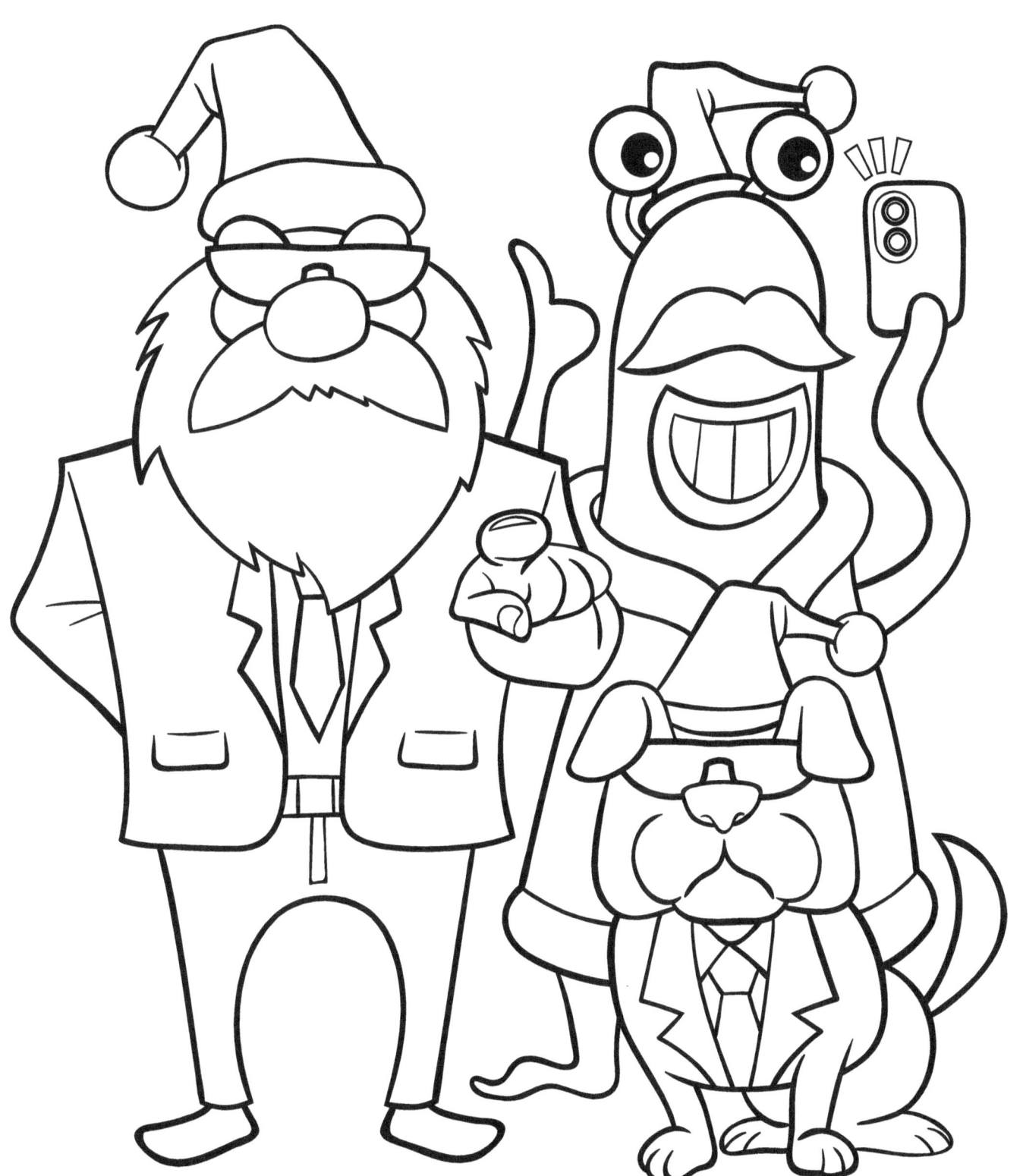

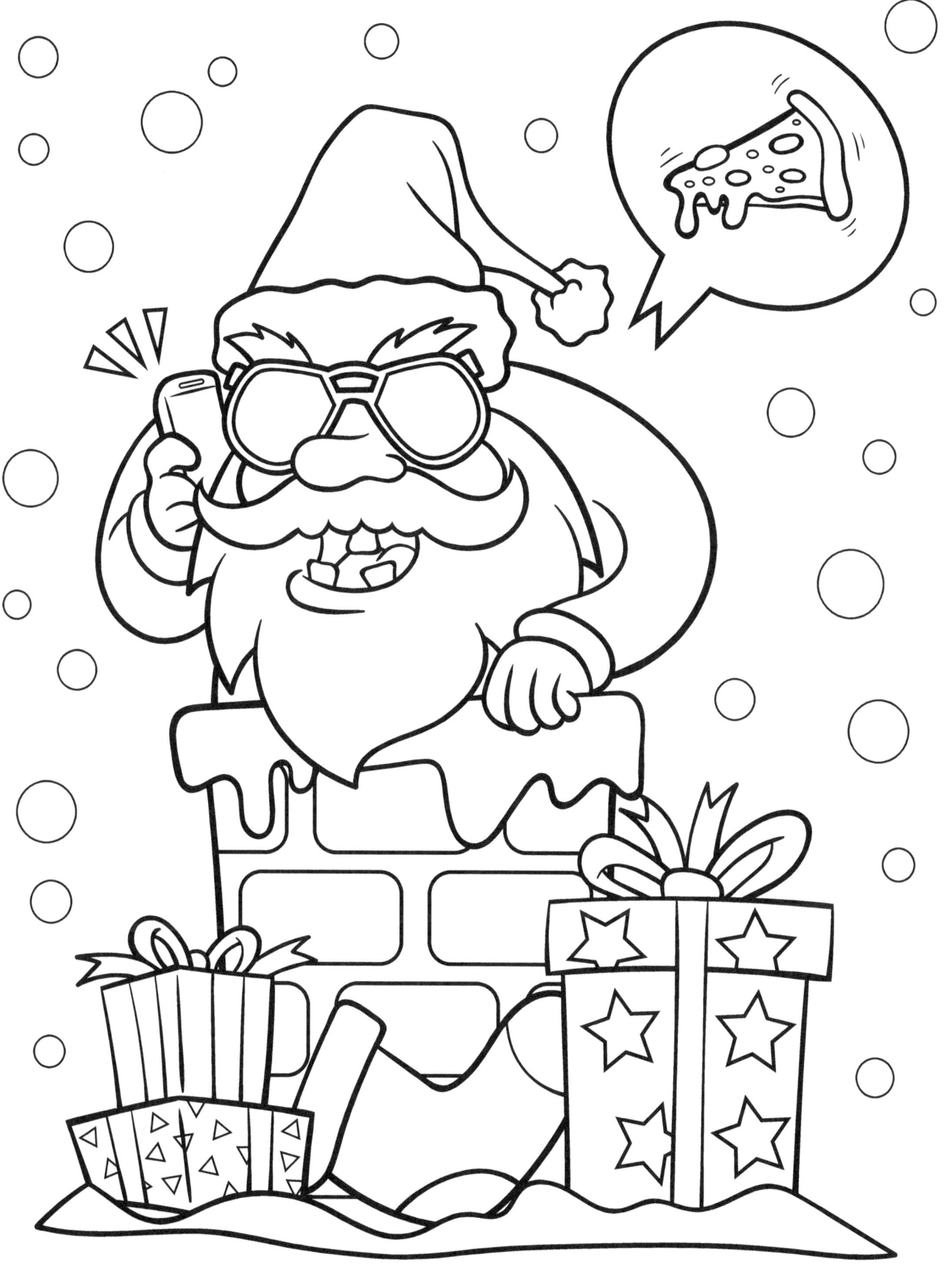

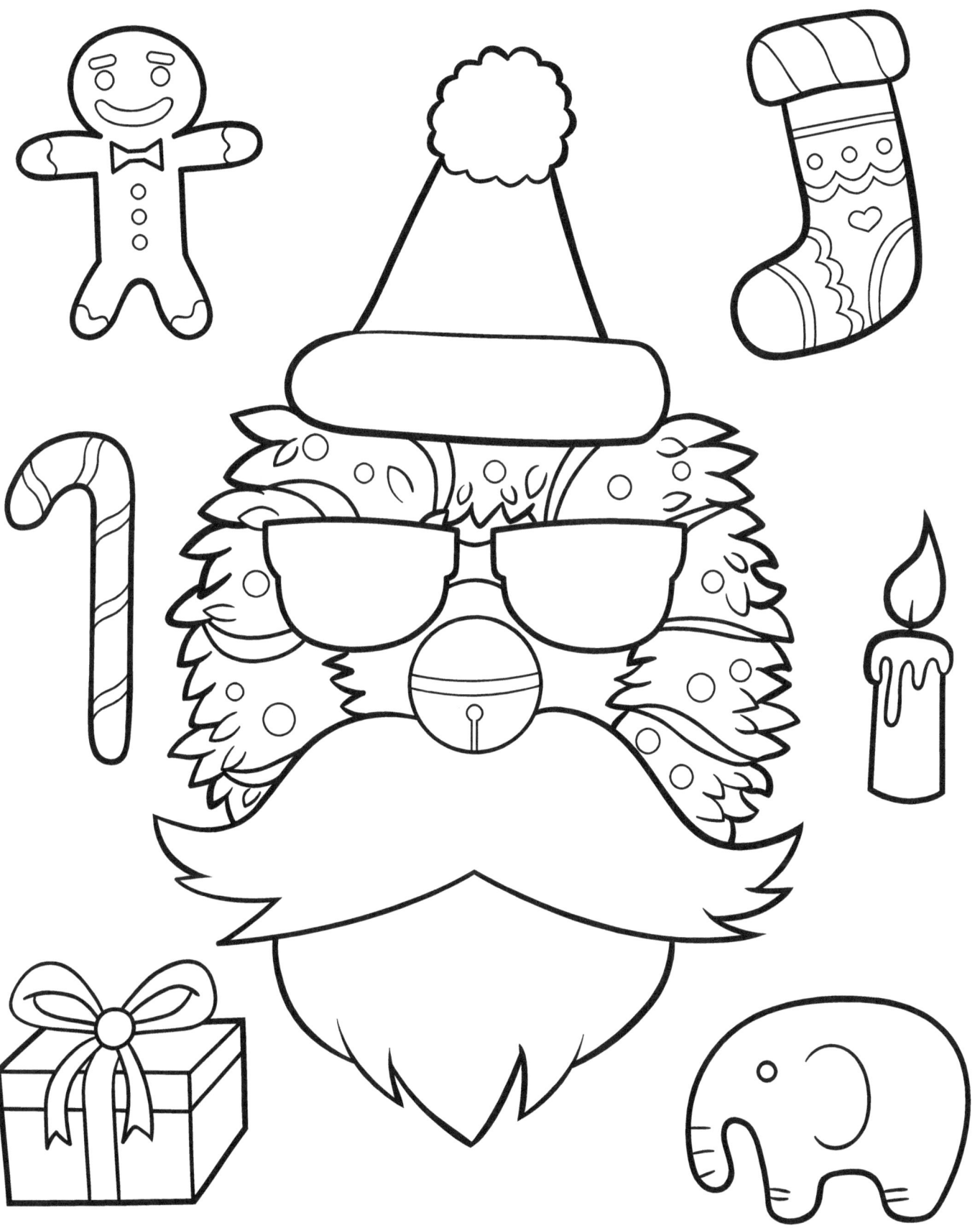

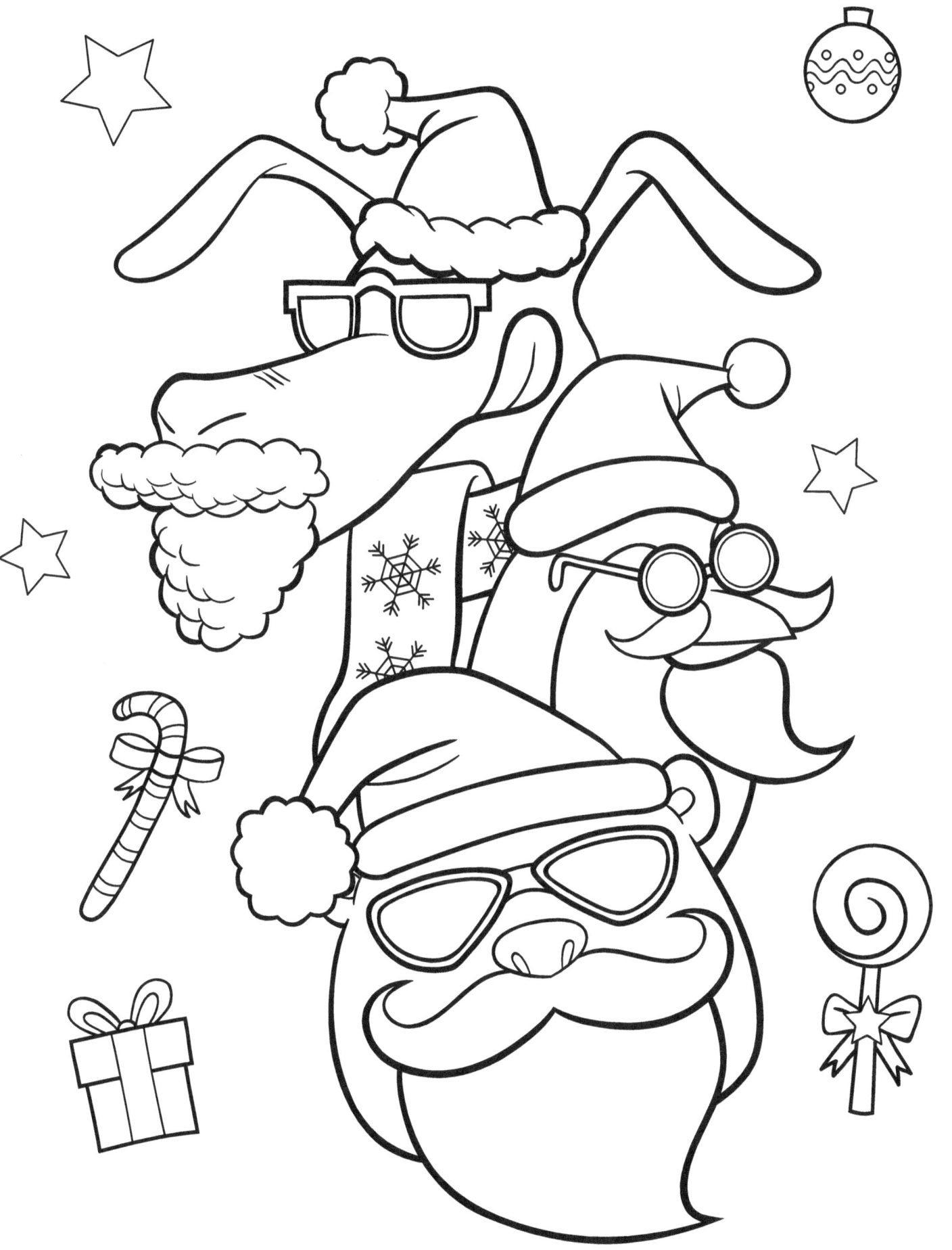

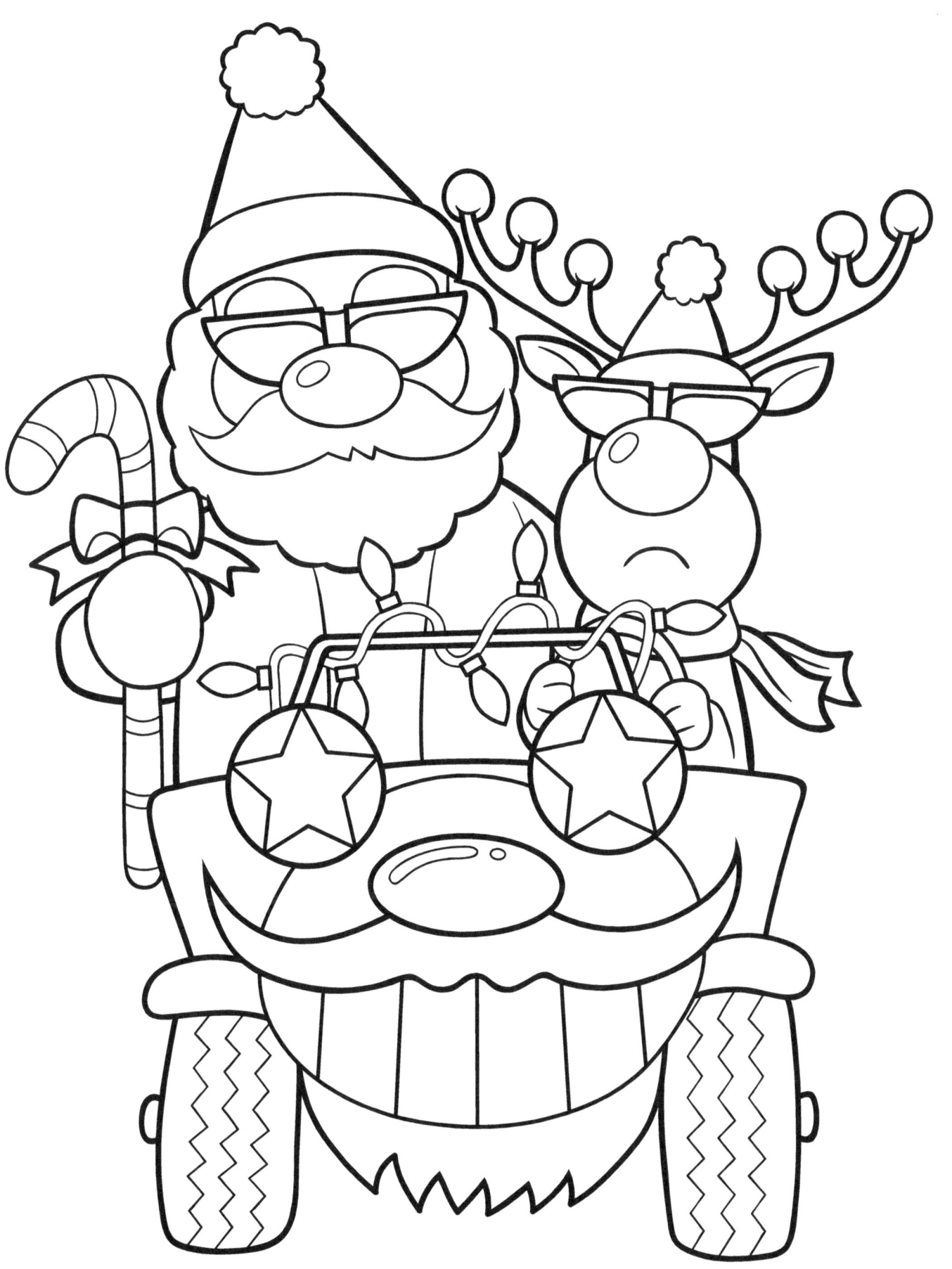

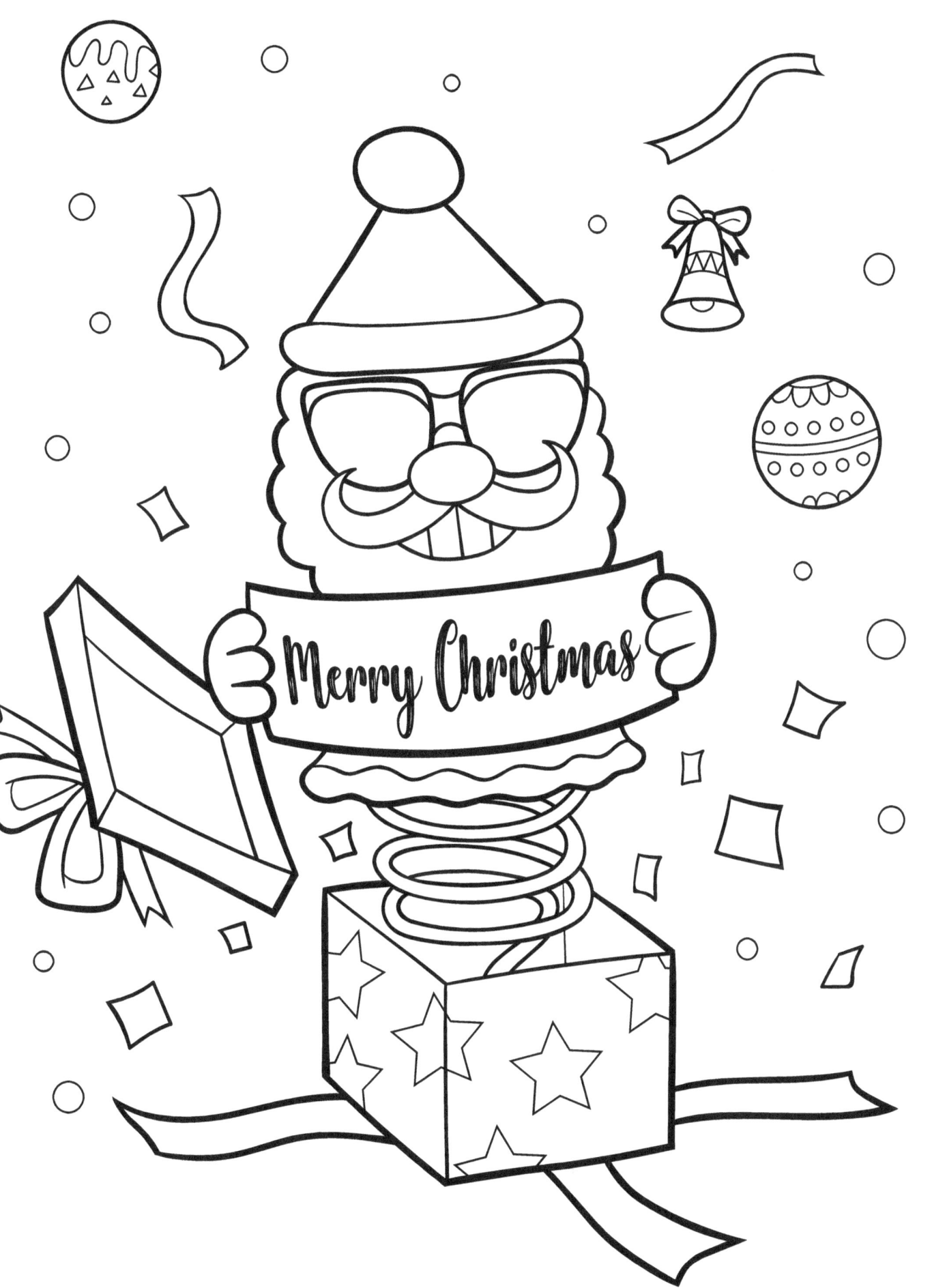

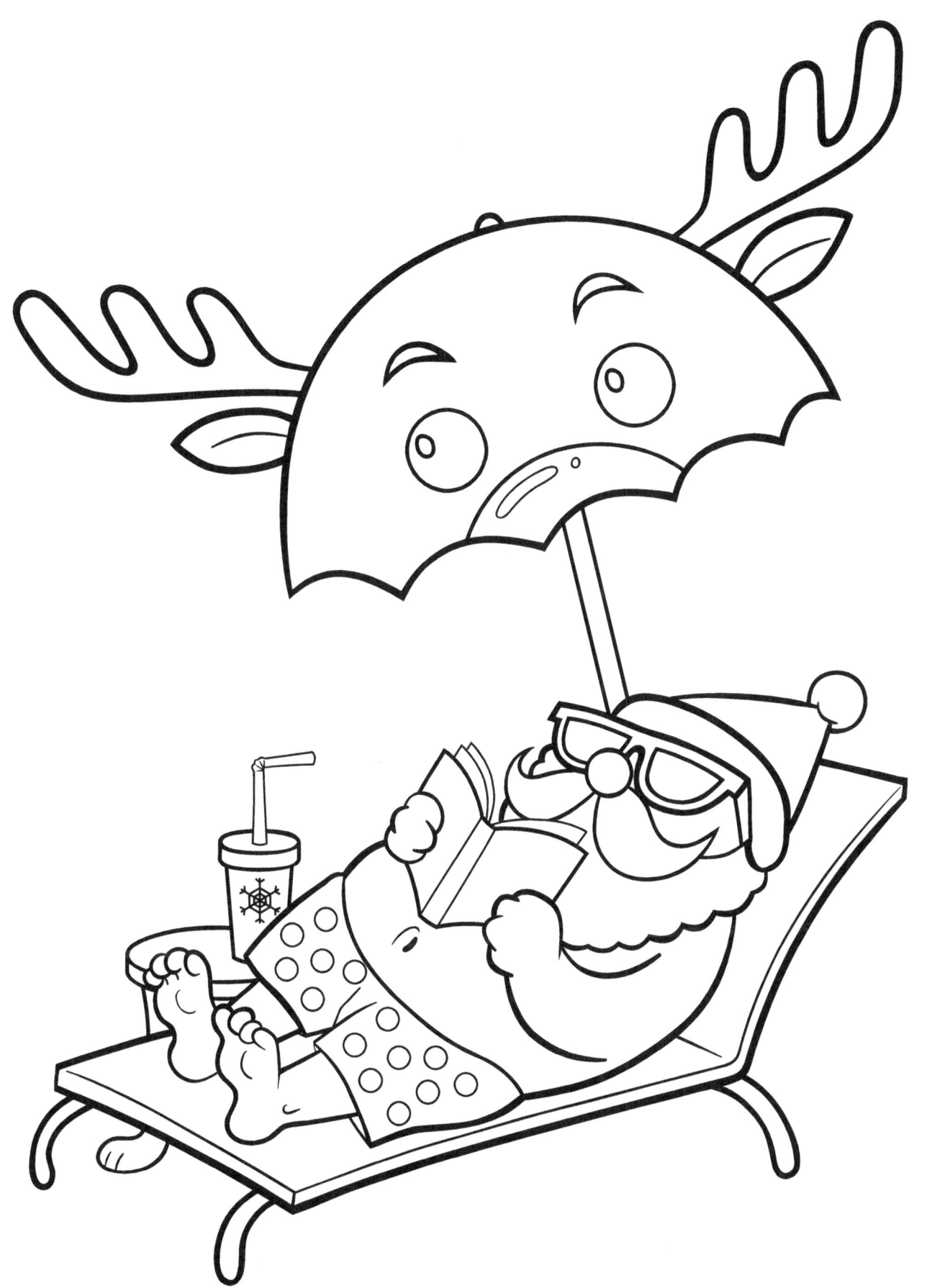

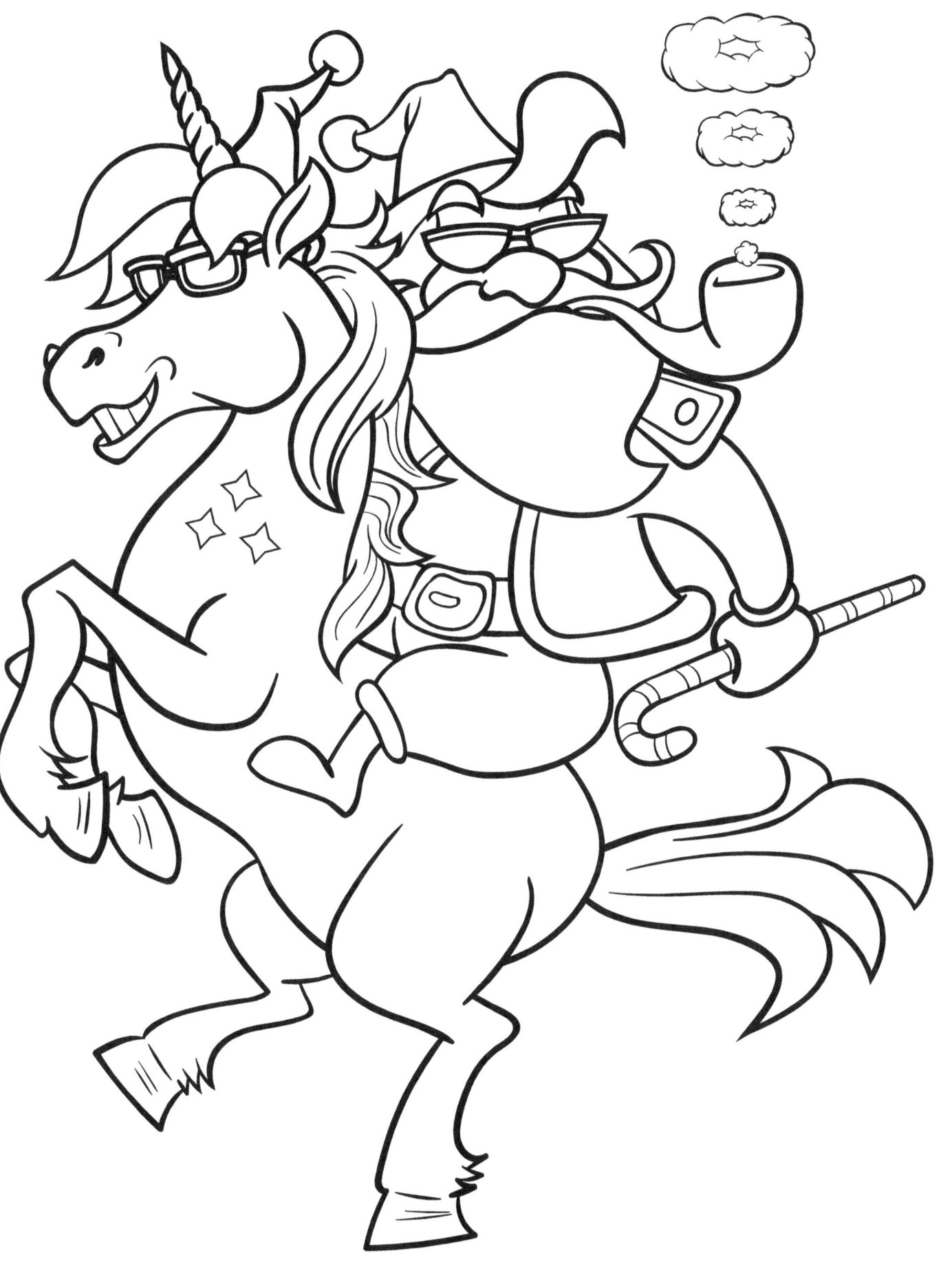

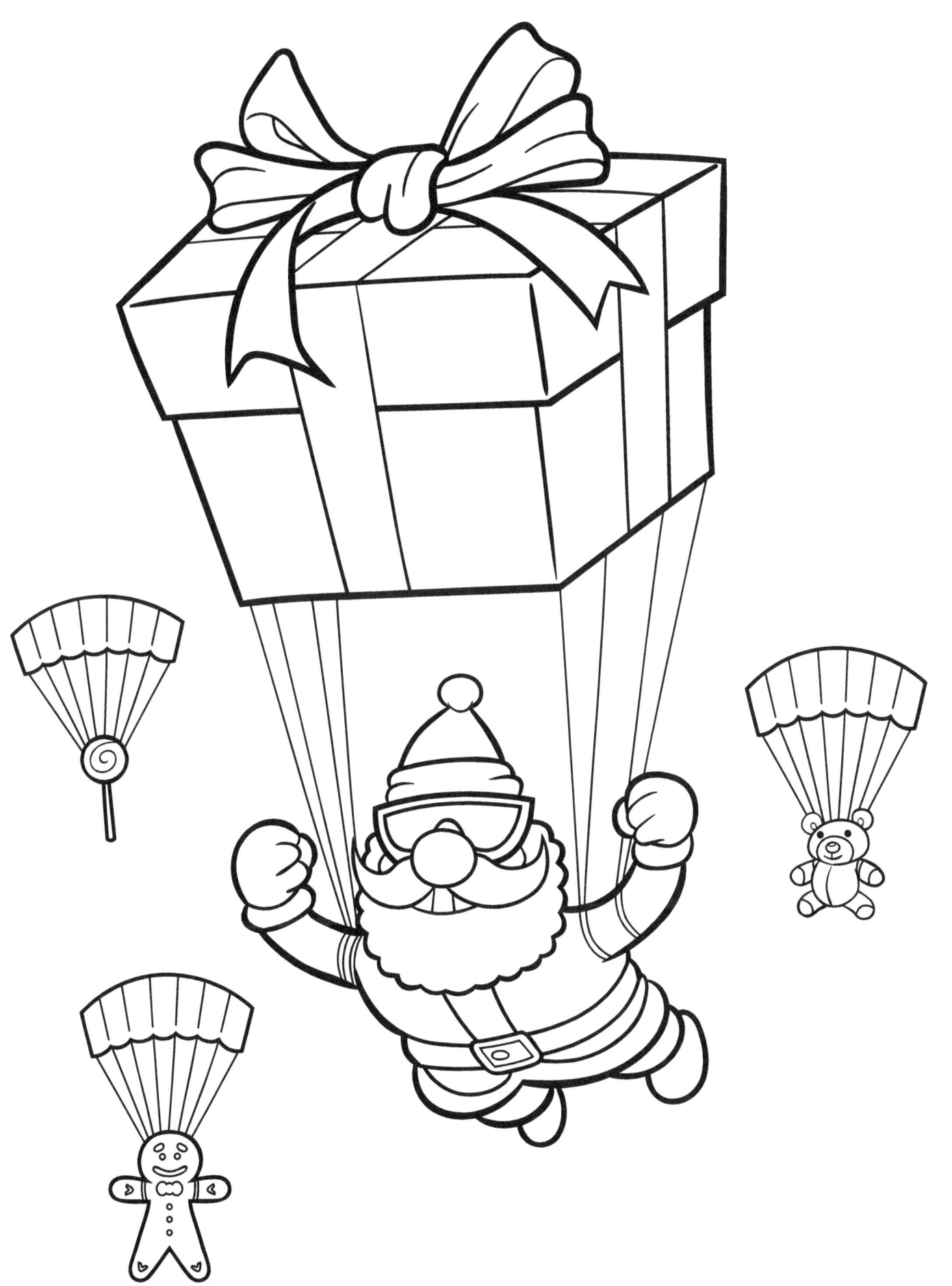

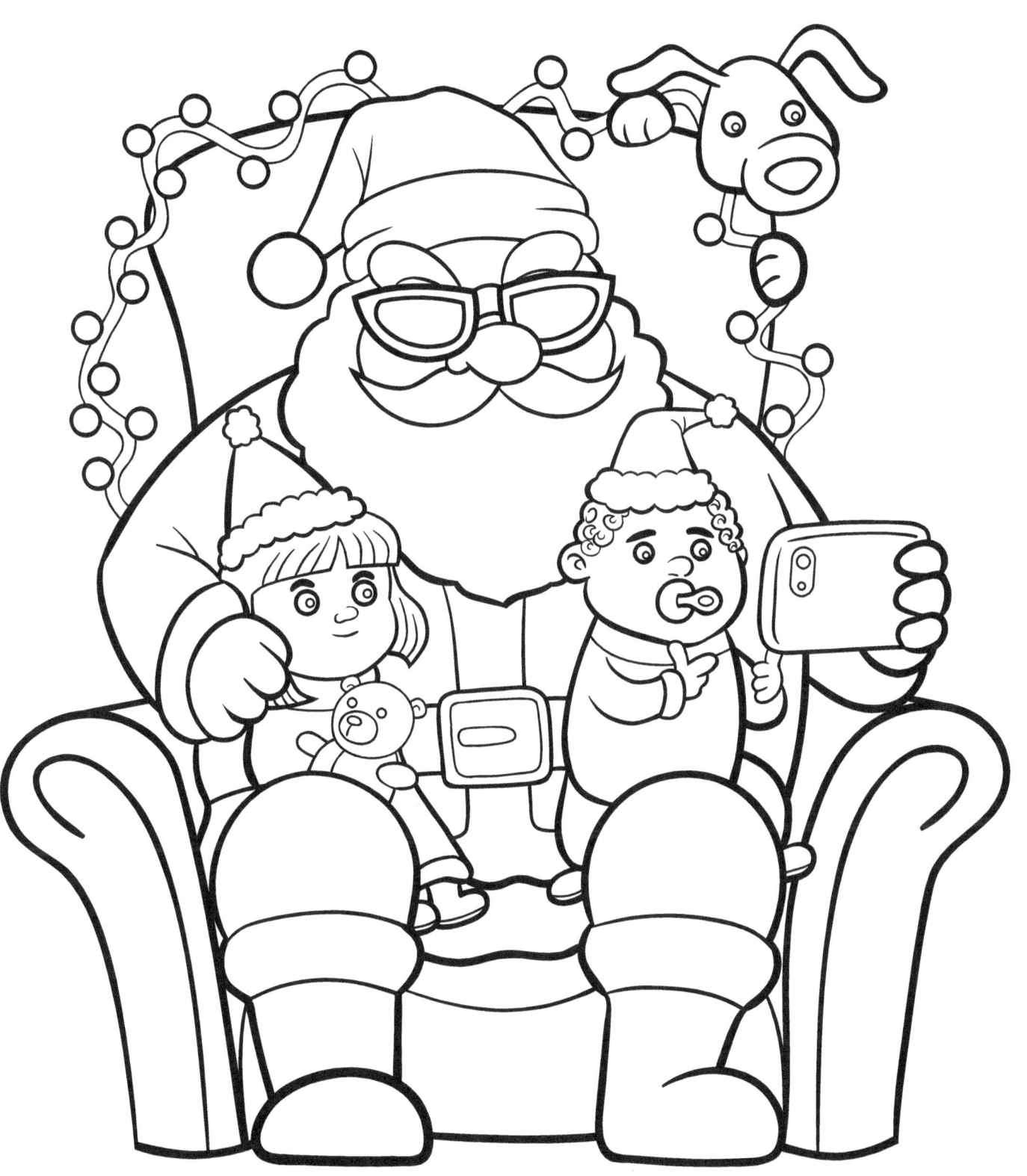

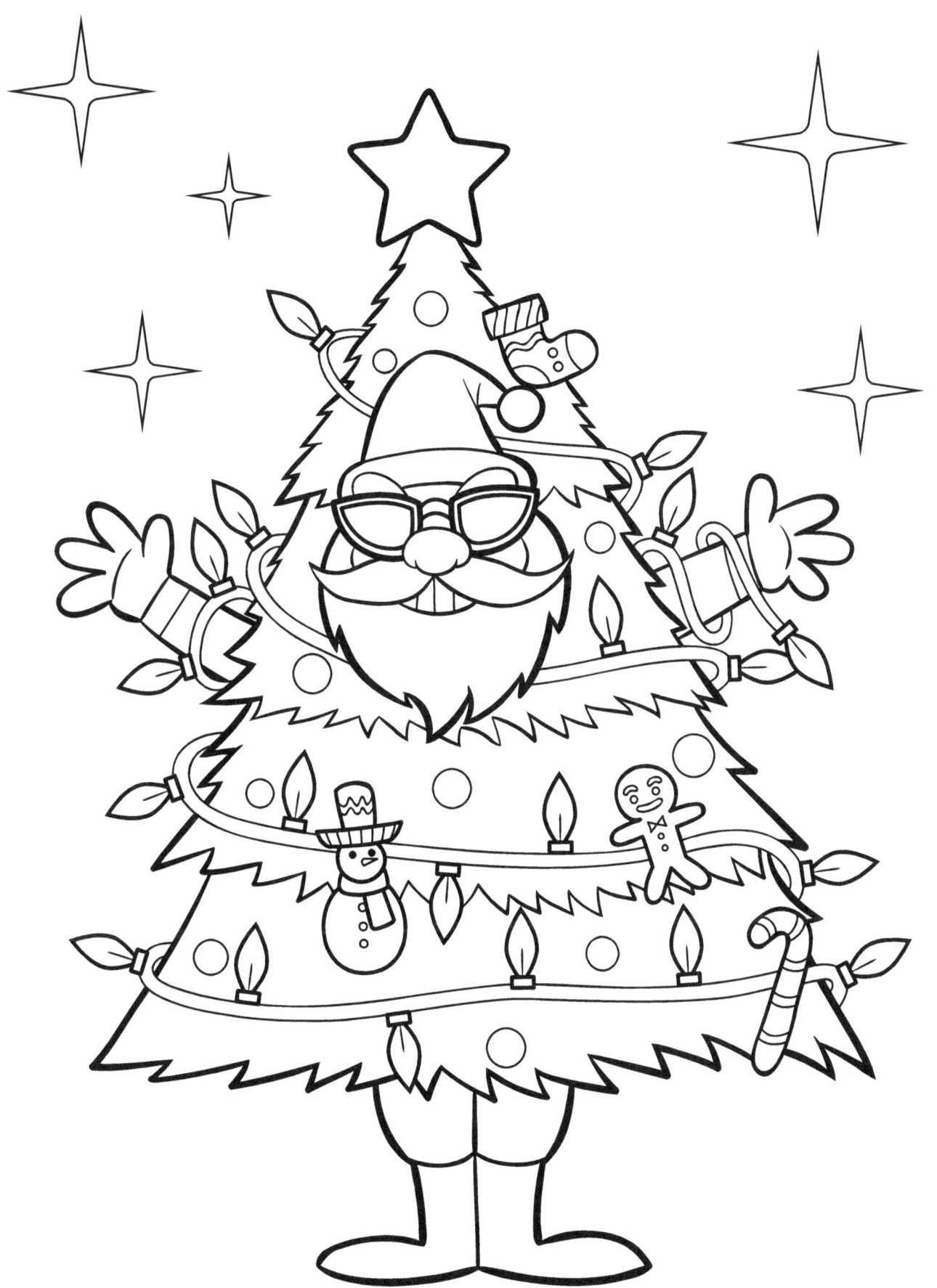

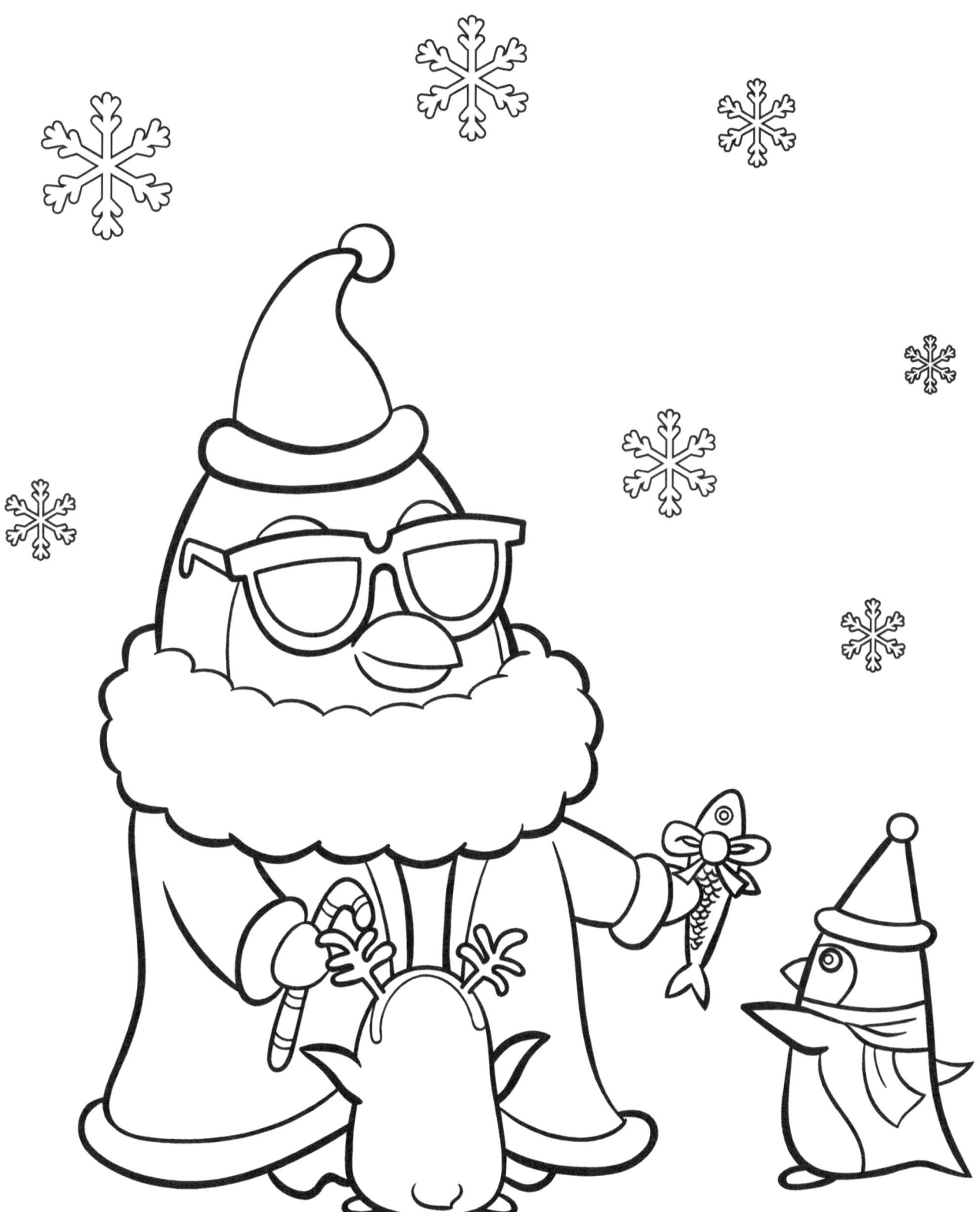

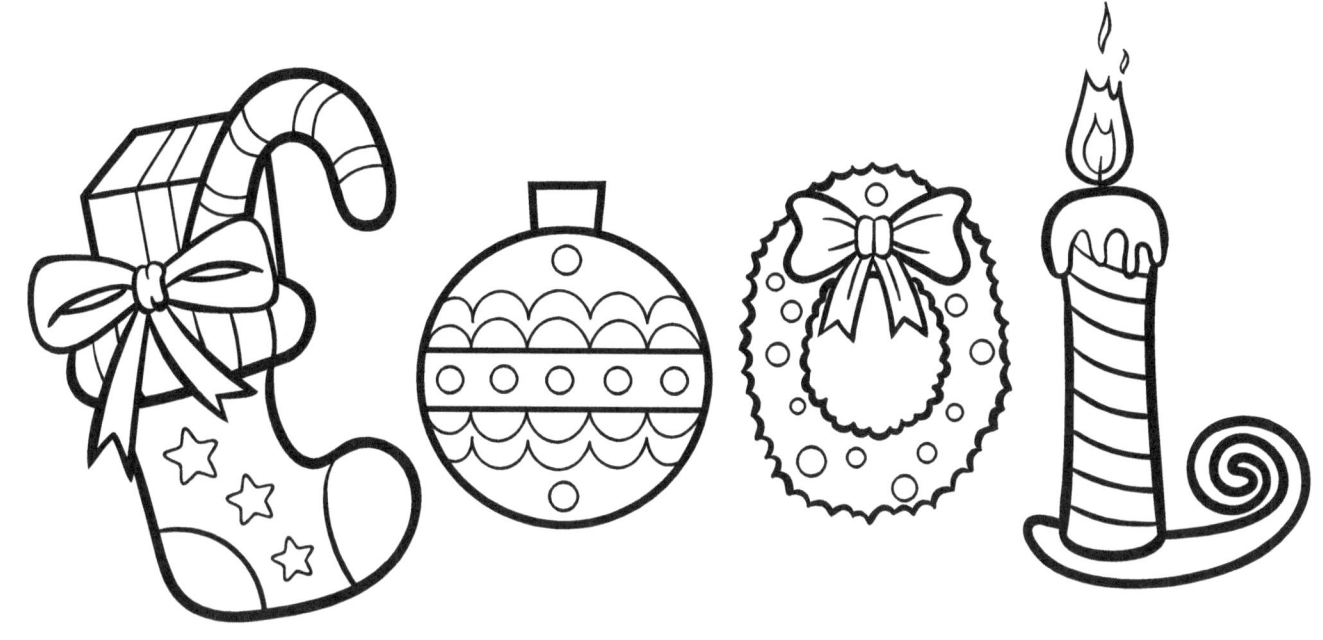

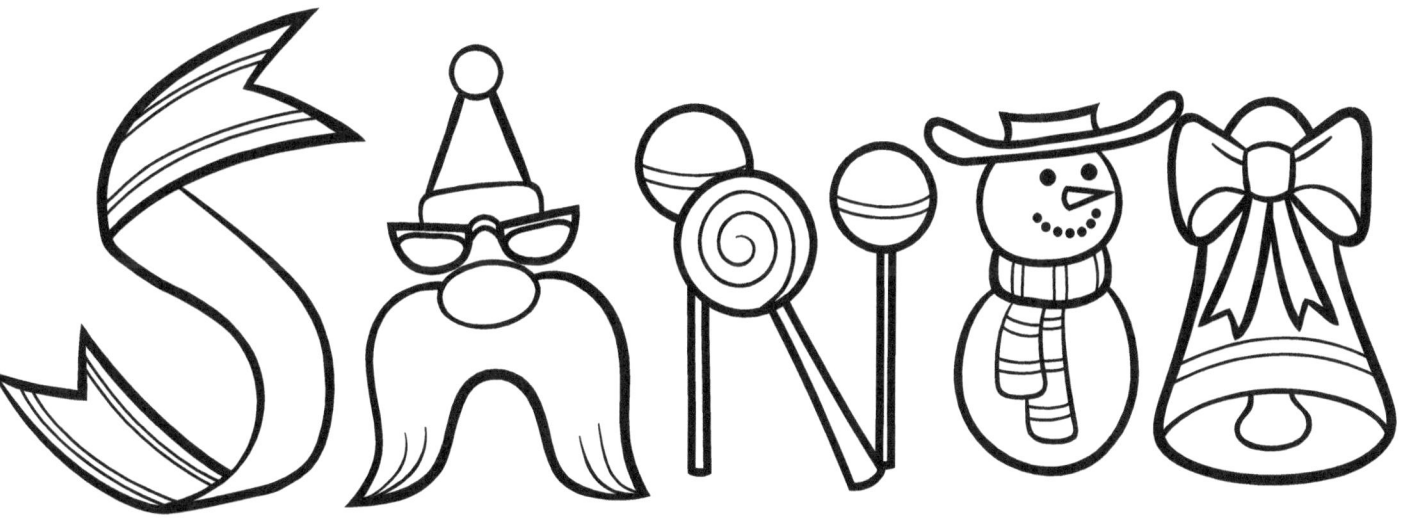